the **NO-NONSENS**

ISLAM

Ziauddin Sardar and Merryl Wyn Davies

the **NO-NONSENSE** guide to

ISLAM

Ziauddin Sardar and Merryl Wyn Davies

To mom,

who might need

this as a reference

'Publishers have created lists of short books that discuss the questions that your average [electoral] candidate will only ever touch if armed with a slogan and a soundbite. Together [such books] hint at a resurgence of the grand educational tradition... Closest to the hot headline issues are *The No-Nonsense Guides*. These target those topics that a large army of voters care about, but that politicos evade. Arguments, figures and documents combine to prove that good journalism is far too important to be left to (most) journalists.'

Boyd Tonkin,
The Independent,
London

guide when you

forget exactly what

you're teaching.

—Sebby

Happy Birthday!

The No-Nonsense Guide to Islam
First published in the UK by
New Internationalist™ Publications Ltd
Oxford OX4 1BW, UK
www.newint.org
New Internationalist is a registered trade mark.

In association with
Verso
6 Meard Street,
London
W1F 0EG
www.versobooks.com

Cover image: Kuwaiti women. Peter Turnley/Corbis

Series Editor: Troth Wells
Design by New Internationalist Publications Ltd.

Typeset by Avocet Typeset, Chilton, Aylesbury, Bucks, UK.
Printed by TJ International Ltd, Padstow, Cornwall, UK.

British Library Cataloguing-in-Publication Data.
A catalogue record for this book is available from the British Library.

Library of Congress Cataloguing-in-Publication Data.
A catalogue for this book is available from the Library of Congress.

ISBN 1-85984-454-5

the **NO-NONSENSE** guide to

ISLAM

Ziauddin Sardar and Merryl Wyn Davies

VERSO

About the authors
Merryl Wyn Davies is a writer and anthropologist and a former producer of religious programs for the BBC. She is the author of *Introducing Anthropology* and *Knowing One Another: shaping an Islamic anthropology*.

Ziauddin Sardar is a writer, broadcaster and cultural critic. He is the author of *Postmodernism and the Other*, *Orientalism*, and *Islam, Postmodernism and Other Futures*, *The Ziauddin Sardar Reader* and numerous other books.

Davies and Sardar are co-authors of the bestseller *Why do People Hate America?*

Other titles in the series
The No-Nonsense Guide to Globalization
The No-Nonsense Guide to Fair Trade
The No-Nonsense Guide to Climate Change
The No-Nonsense Guide to International Migration
The No-Nonsense Guide to Sexual Diversity
The No-Nonsense Guide to World History
The No-Nonsense Guide to Democracy
The No-Nonsense Guide to Class, Caste and Hierarchies
The No-Nonsense Guide to the Arms Trade
The No-Nonsense Guide to International Development
The No-Nonsense Guide to Indigenous Peoples
The No-Nonsense Guide to Terrorism
The No-Nonsense Guide to World Poverty
The No-Nonsense Guide to HIV/AIDS
The No-Nonsense Guide to Global Media

Foreword

HARDLY A DAY goes by without Islam being in the news. But it is almost always bad news. People around the world watching television or reading newspapers can be forgiven for thinking that Muslims have little to do except engage in acts of terrorism, oppress women and minorities, and engage in mindless and fundamentalist rhetoric.

Yet, as most Muslims believe and the history of Islam shows, Islam emerged as a force for justice, equality, human dignity and the rule of law. It created a fraternity across all cultural and tribal and racial divides. It gave honor and respect to the marginalized in society. It practised, albeit briefly, a system of elections against the prevalent norm of the hereditary right to rule. During the formative phase of its development it also followed a practice of open debate to arrive at a consensus before deciding on issues affecting the community. It emphasized knowledge, learning and human creativity. And produced a civilization noted for its learning and humility as well as tolerance, justice and concern for public interest.

None of this history seems to have any relevance for the Muslim world today. That Islam once produced a 'Golden Age' is only of historic interest. A people rise when they excel in creating ideas and decline when others are able to create better or more powerful ideas. Muslims are no exception to this general rule. The process of decline, which some scholars have traced back to 13th century, began when Muslims assumed that they had solved all human problems that needed to be solved had closed the doors of creative endeavors. Muslim societies have paid a very heavy price for this myopia. The mediocrity, intolerance and despotism that is prevalent throughout the Muslim world can all be traced back to this crucial historic upturn. Just how far Muslims have drifted from Islam's emphasis on thought, education and reasoning can be seen from a single statistic: in Pakistan, some 60 per cent of children get their basic education from the *madrassa* (school) where there is nothing but rote learning and where they learn little except bigotry and fanaticism!

The choices before Islam are stark. If Islam is to have any relevance today it must prove that it can produce a more just, tolerant and peaceful society. The orthodox, as well as various reformist movements, must realize that the goal of recreating the 'Madina of the Prophet' and implementing an 8th century 'Islamic Law' is a recipe for further disasters. Muslims need to understand that implementing the *sharia* (Islamic law) would not empower people but creating a civil society and a just order for humanity might.

The No-Nonsense Guide to Islam is a warts-and-all guide to the complex world of Islam. It is a lucid and concise survey of the rich history and the multifaceted diversity of Islam as well as the trials and tribulations of Muslim people. Sardar and Davies show what Islam has achieved; and what it is capable of achieving. But they also delineate what went wrong and what could still go wrong. And, most importantly, they suggest how both Islam and the West can transform themselves to see each other as fully human and capable of laying the foundation for a just world order. That's just how Muslims should think and write.

Dr Ghayasuddin Siddiqui
Director, The Muslim Institute
London, UK

the **NO-NONSENSE** guide to

ISLAM

CONTENTS

the **NO-NONSENSE** guide to

ISLAM

AS MUSLIM WRITERS, we constantly find ourselves caught in a pincer movement. Our Western friends associate Islam largely with violence and bigotry, despotism and suppression, obstinacy and chaos. Our Muslim friends, on the other hand, emphasize that the very term Islam means peace; they conceive of Islam as a religion that by its very essence is about peace and justice. They look to the example of Prophet Muhammad as a model of love, gentleness, fairness, equality and brotherhood.

The association of Islam with aggression has not been hard to find in recent times.

With the terrorist attacks of 11 September 2001 in New York and Washington this association has reached new heights, or more properly, depths. Our Western friends repeatedly asked: Why are Muslims so violent? How can Islam justify the terrorism of al-Qaeda, the suicide bombers in Palestine, the whippings and beheadings under Islamic Law in Saudi Arabia, or stoning to death of adulterers in Nigeria? From these headlines other more general questions arise. Why do Muslims doggedly ignore human and women's rights? Why is democracy in the Muslim world conspicuous by its general absence? Why are Muslims still living in the Middle Ages? And the all round favorite: Is there a clash of civilizations? Have the Muslims declared *jihad* (righteous struggle) against 'Western infidels'? These are highly pertinent questions. Yet, on the whole, Muslims tend to ignore, evade or side step such issues with various forms of apologia. They concentrate on representing the ideals Islam seeks to implement. For example, the famous Muslim scholar Muhammad Asad, a German convert to Islam who produced one of the most respected commentaries on the Qur'an, describes Islam as the 'middle way', the way of balance and tolerance; and of 'liberalism' founded on 'the conception that man's original nature is essentially good'.[1] 'At a fundamental level,' writes Omid Safi, a self-declared 'progressive' Muslim scholar, 'Islamic tradition offers a path to peace, both in the hearts of the individual and the world at large. The actions of these terrorists do not represent real Islam.'

But what is 'real Islam'? When confronted with the reality of terrorist attacks, or the authoritarianism so evident in Muslim states such as Saudi Arabia or the Sudan, or the oppression of women in places like Afghanistan and Pakistan, Muslims have tended, conventionally, to point towards history. 'Just look at our glorious history to see what real Islam is all about,' they say. Indeed, Muslim history, which begins in 610 AD when Prophet Muhammad commenced his career as a prophet in the city of Mecca, in modern-day Saudi Arabia, does present a different picture of Islam. Classical Muslim civilization was progressive. The initial rapid expansion of Islam beyond Arabia was one of the most amazing sequences of events in human history. The emergence of a series of empires in Muslim lands is also a record of the growth of a culture of cities which produced a flowering in arts and sciences that played a major role in the heritage of human ideas. From the 8th to 16th centuries, cities like Baghdad, Damascus, Cairo, Samarkand and Timbuktu were renowned for extensive and elaborate networks of libraries, bookshops, public baths, and hospitals. Experimental method, and thus science as we know it today, was born here. Philosophy was rescued from oblivion, critiqued, extended and expanded. And in

Muslim Spain a genuine multicultural society emerged, where Muslims, Christians and Jews participated in a *convivencia* (the Spanish term for living side by side in harmony).

The trouble is that all this is history. It is far temporally and in temperament from contemporary Islam. How do we reconcile the theoretical ideals of Islam and the progressive glories of history with the situation of the contemporary Muslim world? This question is as important for Muslims as non-Muslims. The Muslim world today is beset by acute problems. It is composed of zones of devastation: large sections of the world's Muslims are among the world's poorest people. It is checkered with zones of conflict where civil war, inter-ethnic fighting, insurgency and terrorism contribute to and compound poverty while ensuring most of the world's refugees are Muslims. There are zones of plenty, oil-rich states where abundance manages to secure continued dependence on Western expertise rather than sponsor self-reliance or generate a new flowering of culture and future possibilities. Across the Muslim world there is populist clamor for Islam, but a dearth of pragmatic thinking and search for solutions derived from the ethos and worldview of Islam. Islam is offered as an antidote to the plethora of problems, but signally fails to galvanize Muslims to solve their own problems. Where there is need or conflict, as much as where there is plenty, Muslims have little confidence in their own polities, nor are their low expectations disappointed. It is a common reflex to blame the West for the genesis of their troubles while at the same time turning to the West in the expectation that solutions to home-grown afflictions will nevertheless be forthcoming.

Contemporary Islam, it has to be said, is not one thing. Its diversity is legendary – not only are there numerous and varied Islamic cultures, but there are also abundant (and competing) interpretations, Schools of Thought, sects and political, apolitical and mystical groups. The term 'Islamic' can be applied to, and is employed by, a vast complex that extends from spiritual practices, mosques and minarets to styles of dress, forms of human behavior, economic practices, political ideas, modes of resistance, philosophy and literature as well as a diversity of social and political movements that exist and affect the affairs of the world today. On one hand this diversity prevents Muslims co-operating and co-ordinating efforts to resolve the evident problems afflicting their societies.

And yet on the other hand populist clamor for Islam, the clarion calls and rhetoric of radical Islamic movements, even earnest debates among well-intentioned concerned Muslim intellectuals all concentrate on the idea there is a unitary, even uniform Islam that should be applied to all situations, circumstances and problems. Resort to this imagined uniformity operates by denying the diversity of Muslim history and the complexity of contemporary life and ends by compounding existing problems.

For Muslims, Islam matters; faith continues to be meaningful. The difficulty is in debating and expressing this faithful confidence as a balanced approach to unity-in-diversity, and as a practical remedy for the multiple problems and multiplicity of problems faced by Muslims.

What we can say with certainty is that Islam today is in need of urgent reforms. And this is important not just for Muslims but for non-Muslims as well. Islam is the world's second largest religion with an estimated 1.3 billion adherents. Every fifth person on the planet is a Muslim. Islam is also a complex of geography and culture, a world civilization. The Muslim world extends from Morocco to Indonesia and from Kazakhstan in Central Asia to the coastal regions of Kenya and Tanzania in Africa. There are substantial Muslim minorities in Europe, Australia and North America. So what the Muslims say and do, how they attempt to solve their problems, how they reform or do not reform Islam, has a direct bearing on all of us.

Thus, what happens to Islam and within Islam will not only affect Muslims, it will shape all our futures. The ability to reform Islam, to expand current debates, to find new approaches and turn away from pathological tendencies confronts everyone with the challenge of understanding how Islam is to make visible the scope and potential Muslims have to make a better future.

Ziauddin Sardar and *Merryl Wyn Davies*

1 M Asad, 'The Sprit of Islam' in *Islam: Its Meaning and Message* edited by Khurshid Ahmad (Islamic Foundation, Leicester, 1975, p 51).

1 Islam: the Qur'an and Sirah

Islam is one of the great religions of the world with some 1.3 billion adherents. But it is also a tradition and culture, a civilization with a long and distinguished history. And it is a worldview – a way of looking at and shaping the world. To see Islam as only one of these components is to miss the whole picture.

HISTORICALLY, ISLAM BEGINS with the Qur'an, the written record of the Revelation made to Prophet Muhammad over a 23-year period from 610 to 632 AD. The Qur'an is the sacred book of Islam. Knowing it is the basis of being a Muslim; it is the direct revelation of God to Prophet Muhammad who lived his entire life in the shadow of the Qur'an. Together with the *Sirah* (the story of his life) the two texts – one written, one lived – constitute the fundamental sources of Islam. Reciting the opening verse, the *Fatihah*, and at least one other is the basis of each cycle in the five daily prayers offered by Muslims.

The language of the Qur'an is itself taken as proof of its divine origin. It uses a distinctive heightened form of Arabic unlike any other Arabic text. Even for native speakers of Arabic reading the Qur'an is a challenge and the majority of Muslims around the world are not native Arabic speakers. The majesty of the use of language in the Qur'an has great beauty and power to move listeners. Indeed, converts to Islam during the time of the Prophet Muhammad were often influenced directly by the language of the Qur'an. Yet the use, structure and expression of language also make it relatively easy to memorize: millions of people around the world, known as *hafiz*, have committed the entire Qur'an to memory. Today, Qur'anic recitation competitions are held all over the Muslim world; public readings, records and tapes of noted recitations are popular with Muslims everywhere.

Wrestling with the meaning of the words of the Qur'an has been a basic part of Muslim scholarship and teaching from the outset. Maintaining and preserving its original text has been a priority for the Muslim community not only to ensure the survival of the text as a whole, but also because the precise form of the words and the use of grammar have significance in understanding its message. This concern to maintain the integrity of original words explains why no translation of the Qur'an is acceptable to Muslims. Numerous translations exist in many languages, but they are regarded as paraphrases, approximations that place the reader a step further from the struggle to appreciate the significance of the Arabic word itself. The Qur'an is the enduring beginning and reference point; all schools of thought, all Muslim discourse of ideas, reform and change, are grounded in this one unitary text. It is the unity from which all diversity derives and by which it is validated. It was and is the basis of education in the narrow sense of religious learning, the education of those who studied what are called the religious sciences and Islamic law. But it was – and is – also the basis of education for those who went on to specialize in studying science, medicine and the arts. In a profound and extensive way Islam is the religion of the Book, the *Kitab*, the Qur'an.

The Qur'an describes itself as an instruction, a teaching and guidance. Its message is addressed to all of humanity; and in particular to 'people who think'. Again and again, it asks its readers to observe, reflect and question. Then it devotes considerable space to delineating the attributes of God. Throughout, the Qur'an stresses knowledge and reason as the valid ways to faith and God-consciousness. Surprisingly, it contains very few legal injunctions.

The Qur'an is composed of 114 chapters, or *surahs*, of varied length. Its structure often perplexes non-Muslims and has caused a great deal of controversy in

Western scholarly circles. Unlike the Bible, it is not structured as a linear narrative, nor are its verses arranged in chronological order according to the sequence in which they were revealed. It is often said that the long opening chapters are concerned with presenting the externals of faith – the details of how to live – while the short concluding chapters are concerned with the inner substance of faith, worship and spiritual verities. Yet even this broad distinction, which has been described as taking the reader on a journey from the 'what' and 'how' to the ultimate question, the 'why', is only an approximation of the way in which the Qur'an arranges its themes. Its subject matter includes events in the life of Prophet Muhammad and the circumstances of the community in which he lived; it introduces stories of previous Prophets; it uses metaphors, allegories and parables and returns to the same topic or theme a number of times. In this way, by instance and restatement, the Qur'an draws out, expands and adds layers of significance to elucidate its meaning and purpose. It is not so much episodic as an interrelated text concerned to make meaningful connections.

The Qur'an consciously declares itself in the circumstances of a particular history and its content is overtly concerned with historical events. But the Qur'an is not a narrative; rather a commentary on the meaning and implications of human history. It questions the past to illuminate and point to a deeper understanding of both spiritual and material truth. Its emphasis on history has had an immense effect on Muslim consciousness. From the outset Muslims have seen the historic circumstances of the Prophet's life and the social setting, time and place of Revelation as essential companion pieces that must be studied to aid understanding the Qur'an.

Muslims believe the Qur'an to be inviolable. The integrity of its text is preserved for all time. Its special structure, the interlocking character of each word and

Some verses from the Qur'an

God loves those who judge equitably. (5:42)

God loves the patient. (3:145)

And one of His signs is the creation of heaven and earth and the diversity of your languages and colors; surely there are signs in this for the learned. (30:22)

Even if you stretch out your hand against me to kill me, I shall not stretch out my hand to kill you. I fear Allah, the Lord of the World. (5:28)

Whosoever does a good deed, male or female, believing – those shall enter paradise, therein provided without reckoning. (40:40)

Take to forgiveness and enjoin good and turn aside from the ignorant. (7:199) ∎

verse, the nature and precision of its heightened language, the economy and subtlety of its style – all make the Qur'an 'inimitable'. Even the minutest change, a dot or a comma, renders the text out of sync. Whenever a verse of the Qur'an was revealed, the Prophet would recite the verse and teach it to his followers. The Prophet himself was unable to read or write as were many of his followers in what was largely an oral society. He was attended by a number of scribes or secretaries, such as Zayd ibn Thabit, who would write down the revealed verses. The Prophet would also indicate exactly where each verse belonged in relation to the others, and thus its place in the Qur'an. Just before his death, the Prophet recited the complete Qur'an to the Muslim community on a number of occasions. After his death, the written text of the Qur'an was given for safe-keeping to one of his wives, Hafsa. As the Muslim community rapidly expanded to new regions there was concern that inauthentic texts were beginning to circulate. Caliph Othman bin Affan, the third successor to Prophet

Calligraphy

The visual art most closely associated with the Qur'an is calligraphy. To the untrained eye what may appear as abstract patterns or elaborate decoration on wall hangings or as part of the fabric of buildings are often in fact Qur'anic texts. This one reads: *A Bismillah* – 'In the name of God, the Beneficent, the Merciful'.

Muhammad as leader of the Muslim community, established a committee to produce an official, authorized written Qur'an. Between the years 650-52 AD this committee, headed by Zayd ibn Thabit, gathered all the extant original materials, consulted with those who had regularly listened to the Prophet recite the Qur'an and produced the text that has been known and used by all Muslims subsequently. Copies of this official text were made and sent to all the major Muslim cities after a recall of all versions previously in circulation. Muslim confidence in the integrity, honesty and scrupulous attention to detail of this process is unshakable.

While the Qur'an is considered by Muslims to be uncreated, a divine gift, Prophet Muhammad is unquestionably human. Both in language and style, his words and sayings are entirely distinct from the Qur'an, and are never confused by Muslims. As the recipient of Revelation, the Prophet is the best guide on its meaning, the best example of its essence and spirit and of how the *din* of Islam (the teachings of religion as a way of life) should be applied and lived. The biography of Prophet Muhammad, known as *Sirah*, also provides information on the historic context in which the Qur'an appeared. The circumstances and conditions of the Prophet's life and the community in which he lived are used to understand the purpose and intention of the principles and regulations contained in the Qur'an. Thus, the *Sirah* is regarded as the second fundamental source of Islam after the Qur'an.

The *Sirah*

Prophet Muhammad was born in 569 AD in Mecca, a city surrounded by rugged mountains that form a chain parallel to the western coast of what is today Saudi Arabia. Mecca was situated on the caravan routes that from antiquity were part a global system of trading connections spanning the known world.

Southwards it was connected to the ports of the Red Sea and coasts of the peninsula linked to Africa and the trading world of the Indian Ocean; northward the trade routes were connected with the cities of Jordan, Palestine, Syria and the Mediterranean coast, the world of ancient Middle Eastern as well as Hellenic and Roman civilizations. The people of Mecca were traders and the city itself was an important trading center as well as a center of pilgrimage drawing people from the whole of pre-Islamic Arabia.

The Prophet's father, Abdullah, died around the time of his birth while on a commercial trip to Yathrib, the city that later became Medina. His mother, Amina, according to local custom, sent her son to be fostered by a wetnurse in the region of Taif. When he returned to his mother aged four years they journeyed to Yathrib where they stayed for two years. Amina died on their return journey to Mecca and Prophet Muhammad was taken in by his grandfather, Abd al-Muttalib, who lived only another two years. The eight-year-old was then placed in the care of his father's full brother, the merchant Abu Talib, helping tend the flocks of a neighbor as well as assisting in his uncle's cloth shop. At the age of nine, the boy accompanied his uncle on a trading expedition to Palestine.

By the age of 24, Prophet Muhammad was responsible for running the business of his aging uncle and had earned himself the surname al-Amin, the honest. Hearing of his reputation, a wealthy widow named Khadijah asked him to take a consignment of her goods to Palestine. He returned with double the expected returns. Khadijah then proposed marriage. It is generally said that not only was Khadijah the wealthier partner but also the elder one as she was 40 when the couple married in 595 AD. However, other reports put Khadijah's age as 28, a fact which might be corroborated by her bearing seven children after the marriage. Of these children, only the four daughters,

Zainab, Ruqaiya, Umm Kulthum and Fatimah survived to adulthood, three boys dying in infancy. On his marriage Prophet Muhammad moved into his wife's household. To lighten the burden on his uncle Abu Talib the couple took in one of his sons, Ali, who would later become the fourth leader of the Muslim community. The Prophet continued to work as a trader, traveling several times to Yemen and once to Oman.

What drew pilgrims from all over Arabia to the Prophet's birthplace Mecca was the *Ka'aba*, a shrine originally built by Prophet Abraham for the worship of the One God. By Prophet Muhammad's time the *Ka'aba* had long become a polytheistic shrine housing statues of 360 deities. In 605 AD the *Ka'aba* was damaged by fire and had to be rebuilt. The last phase of renovation was to install a round black meteorite in the wall of the building. There was considerable dispute among the citizens over which clan should have the honor of setting the Black Stone in place. At this point the Prophet arrived and was asked to settle the dispute. His solution was to place the Black Stone on a cloth. A representative of each clan would then hold the cloth and together they would lift the Stone which he then set in place.

For Prophet Muhammad the rebuilding of the *Ka'aba* began a period of religious reflection. He began to make regular retreats from the city to a cave on nearby Mount Hira where he would spend a month at a time in quiet contemplation. It was on his fifth annual retreat, at the age of 40, during December 609, that he first saw the Angel Gabriel. He was asleep in the cave when the Angel appeared and commanded him to 'Read'. Prophet Muhammad's response was to say simply he could neither read nor write. Despite his protestations, the Angel continued to command the Prophet to 'Read!' Finally, the Prophet asked: 'What shall I read?' The Angel replied:

Read, with the name of Thy Lord, Who has created
Who has created man of a drop of blood!
Read, and thy Lord is most bounteous,
Who has taught by pen:
Who has taught man what he knew not!
(The Qur'an: 96: 1-5).

This was the first revelation to be received by the Prophet, and he found the experience deeply unsettling. He returned home to confide in his wife Khadijah, who consoled and reassured him and accepted the validity of his experience. Khadijah is therefore considered the first person to embrace the new religion and become a Muslim. So begins what is called the Meccan Period, the early phase of Prophet Muhammad's life as the Messenger of Islam.

This formative period opens with his personal struggle to accept the idea of prophethood and initial tentative sharing of his experience with members of his family and closest friends. There were those, such as his friend Abu Bakr and nephew Ali, who accepted that Prophet Muhammad was now a Messenger of God and formed the kernel of a new body of believers. Equally, there were members of the Prophet's family, such as the wife of his uncle Abu Lahab, who were sceptical and soon openly derisive. It was three years after the event in the cave of Hira before a further instance of Revelation. The sequence and dating of each verse of the Qur'an has been meticulously compiled by Muslim scholars and the first halting steps of coming to terms with the enormity of the idea of Revelation features prominently in all biographies of the Prophet.

After the three-year hiatus, when according to al-Bukhari, one of the most authoritative early commentators and compiler of *hadith* (sayings of the Prophet), Prophet Muhammad had almost reached the point of despair, he was called on to proclaim the Message of Islam openly to the people of Mecca. The shift to publicly proclaiming a new religion to the entire community brought friction that developed into open animosity, especially with the powerful Quaraysh clan, and repression. The central message of Islam of the Oneness of God directly contradicts polytheism; and Prophet Muhammad's message and activities were seen as threatening and subversive to the vital interests of the community. The news of his activities spread rapidly across Arabia, again causing concern to the Meccan élite, headed by Abu Sufyan. Pressure was brought to bear on the gradually increasing number of Muslims to recant their new faith. As a member of the Banu Hashim, a prominent clan in Mecca, the Prophet was under the personal protection of the head of that clan, his uncle Abu Talib, despite the fact his uncle never embraced Islam. However, many of the new converts were easier targets. They were physically harassed, beaten, tortured and killed as the powerful of Mecca sought to stifle the new movement in their midst.

In 616 Prophet Muhammad became so concerned at the persecution of his followers he advised some of them to migrate to Abyssinia and seek refuge under the protection of its Christian ruler, the Negus. A group of 80 Muslims made the journey under the leadership of Ja'far ibn Abi Talib. They included the Prophet's daughter Ruqaiya and her husband Othman bin Affan, later the third Caliph or successor to Prophet Muhammad. In Abyssinia the refugees were permitted to practice their faith, and the Negus refused the two emissaries sent by the Quraysh clan to demand the Muslims be rejected as outlaws and returned.

The Prophet and his family remained in Mecca where they were subject to a boycott: nobody was to talk to them, sell to or buy from them or marry among them. Prophet Muhammad, the remaining Muslims and members of his clan moved to a secluded suburb where they were clandestinely supported by sympathetic relatives. The privations caused by this boycott further divided public opinion in Mecca. In 619, a group of citizens openly declared they would no longer support it; so the Prophet's clan was able to return to the city. The hardship and hunger they endured took their toll. In that year both Prophet Muhammad's wife Khadijah and his uncle Abu Talib died. Until her death Khadijah was the Prophet's only wife. After her death he re-married; in all he married 11 women. Many were widows whose husbands had died in the repression or battles of the early Muslim community. One, Safiyah, belonged to a Jewish tribe while his last marriage was to Maryam Qibtiyah who had been raised as an Egyptian Coptic Christian. Both women had converted to Islam before their marriage. All were given a free choice to accept or reject marriage to Prophet Muhammad. The wives of the Prophet became important and occasionally controversial figures in the Muslim community. They played a crucial role in reporting details of the custom, usage and opinions of the Prophet, the traditions which shaped the development of Islamic civilization.

With the death of Abu Talib, leadership of the Banu Hashim clan passed to Abu Lahab, a determined opponent of the Prophet's activities. The Prophet now considered the possibilities of emigrating, making an exploratory visit to Taif, where he had relatives. Shortly after his return he had the vision known as the *Miraj*, literally the ascension, the subject of the Night Journey (chapter 17 of the Qur'an). In this vision Prophet Muhammad was transported from Mecca to Jerusalem and then ascended to heaven into the Divine Presence. During this episode the clear lineaments of the *din* of Islam, religion as a way of life, were set. Some commentators see it as analogous to the Commandments given to Moses. After this event the pattern of five daily prayers as the way of worship was established.

The persecution in Mecca and the search for a new refuge continued. During the pilgrimage of 621 some members of the Khazraj group from the city of Yathrib converted to Islam and agreed to return the following year with an answer on the question of asylum for the Prophet. The following year 500 people from Yathrib attended the pilgrimage – of these, 74, including two women, were Muslims. They sought out the Prophet to declare their conversion to Islam and pledged a pact of allegiance, *bai'a*, to protect the Prophet and invited him and his followers to settle in Yathrib. Soon the *Hijra*, the migration from Mecca, began with small groups of Muslims leaving their native city. The Meccans were enraged at the prospect of the further spread of Islam and vowed to assassinate the Prophet who went into hiding to evade his pursuers.

His departure from Mecca is taken as the start of a new era and the beginning of the calculation of the Muslim calendar, expressed as AH from the Latin *Anno Hegirae*: in the year of the *Hijra*. The new calendar was actually introduced some 17 years after this event, which corresponds to 16 July 622 AD in the Julian calendar. It was instituted by the second Caliph, Umar ibn al-Khattab to provide consistency in dating of correspondence across the expanding Muslim empire.

The *Hijra* marks a major change in the preaching and institutionalizing of Islam as a way of life and living together. The Prophet was acknowledged as the leader of a newly renamed city, Medina. The city had a diverse population composed of a number of groups: the *Ansar*, the Helpers, were natives of Yathrib who extended practical support and aid to the *Muhajars*, the Migrants who had left behind their homes and had their property confiscated by the Meccan authorities. Medina was a heterodox city of Muslims, polytheists as well as Jews. The Prophet convened a general meeting of all citizens and a written agreement was drawn up defining the mutual relations of the various groups. Thus Medina became a political territorial entity of confederated groups: a

Some sayings of Prophet Muhammad

The world is green and beautiful and God has appointed you his trustee over it.

Little, but sufficient, is better than the abundant and the alluring.

The search for knowledge is a sacred duty imposed upon every Muslim.

God is gentle and loves gentleness in all things.

Pay the worker before his sweat dries.

He is not a believer who eats his fill while his neighbor remains hungry by his side.

As you are, so you will have rulers over you.

The special character of Islam is modesty. ■

city-state with a written constitution. It was under threat from the hostility of the Meccans while having to integrate and build a new system covering the whole gamut of civic affairs for its citizens, Muslim and non-Muslim. It is in this context that the 10 years of the Medinan Period unfolds.

The center of community life in Medina was the Prophet's Mosque, where he actually lived. The community would gather at the mosque to discuss their affairs and reach agreement by consensus. From the outset mosques have always been understood as having dual functions, both religious worship and civil, especially social welfare duties. Reports give examples of men and women standing up at these assemblies and questioning the policy and decisions outlined, even those of the Prophet himself. There are examples of questions of marriage and divorce being settled by him, along with the panoply of individual and personal matters of concern to ordinary people coming to terms with the meaning of their new faith as a way of life. Collections of *hadith* (see next chapter), for example, usually have one whole section dealing with women who came to ask the Prophet questions on menstruation, childbirth and breastfeeding. It is in this period that the pattern of religious life was instituted, including the fast from dawn to dusk during the month of Ramadan and the paying of *zakat*, the obligatory 'poor due'.

The Medinan Period also includes the open warfare between Mecca and the new Muslim community. In particular the Prophet participated in three battles. There is an overriding tendency in biography, commentary and general histories, both Muslim and non-Muslim, to concentrate on the battles. Indeed, some Muslim biographies devote the bulk of the *Sirah* to the battles. Yet, collectively they occupied less than a month of the Medinan Period.

The emergence of conflict between Mecca and Medina was hardly surprising. The establishment of Medina as a confederated city-state under the administration of Prophet Muhammad, and which covered territory lying across the routes used by the two annual Meccan trade caravans, clearly impacted on vital Meccan economic interests. The battles were decisive in determining the continued existence of the fledgling Islamic community and created the conditions for its rapid expansion. The first, the Battle of Badr, took place in 624. Badr is a small town about 85 miles southwest of Medina on the caravan route connecting Mecca to Damascus. Here a force of 950 Meccans, dispatched to protect a caravan, engaged 300 Muslims. In a fierce battle that lasted less than a day, 45 Meccans including their leader Abu Jahl and a number of other prominent citizens were killed and 14 Muslims lost their lives.

The following year, the Meccans mobilized a force of 3,000 for an assault on Medina. Prophet Muhammad mustered about 700 Muslims and a pitched battle took place near the hill of Uhad just north of Medina. Rather than part of a concerted, ongoing war, the Battle of Uhad has all the marks of a traditional revenge raid. After initially repelling the Meccan force, the Muslims were thrown into disarray by an attack from the rear. In the fighting the Prophet was wounded, adding to the confusion. Seventy Muslims were killed while the Meccans lost 20 men. Among the Muslims killed was Hamza, Prophet Muhammad's uncle whose body was mutilated by Hind, the wife of Abu Sufyan, in revenge for her father whom Hamza had killed at Badr. When the day's fighting ended, the attacking force returned to Mecca.

In 627 a Meccan army of 10,000 laid siege to Medina in what is known as the Battle of the Trench, so called after the defensive ditch Prophet Muhammad had dug to protect his city. Repeated attempts to cross the ditch failed and after two weeks the Meccan army, dispirited by bad weather, failing supplies and internal dissension, decided to withdraw. This attempt to overthrow the new community resulted in ten fatalities on both sides. It clearly dented the prestige of the Meccans and added to the growing confidence of the Muslim cause. In the aftermath of the Battle, the Prophet sent 500 gold coins to be distributed among the poor of Mecca where a famine was underway. He also sent a large quantity of dates to Abu Sufyan and asked in exchange to barter the stock of hides which Abu Sufyan could not export. The reports of these events make it clear that women accompanied and supported both sides in each of the battles.

In 628, the Prophet announced his intention to make a pilgrimage to the *Ka'aba* (the sacred focus of Islam; see chapter 2) in Mecca and arrived with a group of about 1,600 people. When he reached Hudaybiya on the outskirts, he sent an envoy requesting permission to enter Mecca in peace for a few days. This request was denied by the Meccans but an agreement, the Treaty of

Hudaybiya, was declared. The Prophet would be permitted to make the pilgrimage the following year and the parties agreed to remain neutral should either city be engaged in conflict with a third party.

The Meccans did not stick to their side of the bargain making several infringements of the Treaty. So, in 630 Prophet Muhammad gathered together a force some 10,000 strong and marched on Mecca. On his approach, the city immediately surrendered and he re-entered his birthplace without fighting. The city elders were brought to the Prophet and stood in front of him. These were the people who for 21 years had opposed and persecuted him, tortured and killed his followers, and eventually drove him out of the city. The Prophet asked 'What do you expect of me now?' Then he answered his own question: All your crimes are forgiven; 'there is no responsibility on you any more today. Go, you are liberated.' This magnanimity shook the Meccans and many then embraced Islam, including their leader Abu Sufyan. The *Ka'aba*, which contained numerous statues, was cleared of its idols and rededicated to the worship of One God. Prophet Muhammad returned to Medina and no Muslim force was left in Mecca.

The fall of Mecca quickened the spread of Islam across the whole of Arabia. Not all the people of Arabia become Muslims but the authority of Muslim government was recognized by all. Initial contacts were made with the powerful empires, Byzantine and Persian, on the borders of Arabia. The Prophet wrote to their leaders inviting them to Islam. Throughout the Medinan Period religious and civic affairs were concentrated in the person of Prophet Muhammad and he was now surrounded by a growing body of secretaries. In 632 the ailing Prophet made his farewell pilgrimage (*hajj*) to Mecca. It was during this pilgrimage, on the ninth day of the month of Dhul Hijjah in the year 11 AH that the final verse of the Qur'an was revealed:

> This day have I
> Perfected your religion
> For you, completed
> My favor upon you,
> And chosen for you
> Islam as your religion. (5:3)

The date remains the culmination of the hajj, the annual Muslim pilgrimage to Mecca. During his pilgrimage Prophet Muhammad delivered his final sermon, describing himself as the slave of God and His Messenger, addressing the crowd: 'I enjoin you, O slaves of God, to fear God, and I incite you to obey Him. And I begin with what is good.' What he commends to Muslims is a charter of social justice and equity dealing with actual concerns and tensions of a society in transition, moving from the ways of the 'time of ignorance' to a new set of moral and ethical precepts. It includes seminal phrases: 'Your wives have a right over you and you have a right over them'; 'The believers are only brethren'; 'Your Lord is one, and your ancestor is also one: all of you are descendants of Adam and Adam was made of clay'; 'No Arab has any superiority over a non-Arab'; 'Let the present communicate to the absent.' On completing his hajj the Prophet returned to Medina where he died peacefully a few months later.

The Prophet Muhammad is known to Muslims as The Seal of The Prophets. His death marks the completion of both the fundamental sources of Islam – the Qur'an and *Sirah* – and of all prophethood. From this point Muslim history becomes the struggle of a human community to interpret and implement the teachings of Islam in a changing society.

2 What is Islam?

As a religion, Islam is deceptively simple. Its creed consists of a two-part statement: 'There is no god but God; and Prophet Muhammad is the messenger of God'. Anyone who makes this declaration – known as the *shahadah*, meaning bearing witness – freely and sincerely is a Muslim.

THE *SHAHADAH* BEGINS by negating the existence of false deities and affirming belief in One, Omnipotent, Omniscient, Omnipresent and All Powerful God. God, or Allah, is the absolute Creator and Ruler of the Universe. He 'beggetteth not, nor is He begotten.' Unlike Christianity, Islam rejects the idea that God intervenes in history in human form. No intermediaries are needed and God alone is worthy of worship. Indeed, God has no gender; though, by convention, Muslims use the pronoun, He. He is thus unique and can only be known by finite, human minds through His attributes or names. In Islamic tradition, there are 99 Names of God, beginning with al-Awwal, the First, to al-Akhir, the Last. The most common attributes of God are contained in the statement Muslims utter every time they undertake an action: 'In the name of God, the Beneficent, the Merciful'. The Merciful and Compassionate God is the Forgiving, Nurturing and Sustaining Creator, the Loving, Helper, Giver and Guide from which all creation derives, to whom all creation belongs and ultimately returns.

From this uncompromisingly monotheistic premise, Islamic theology derives a number of logical conclusions. The relationship between God and His creation, men and women, is that of dependence. Every individual has a direct relationship with God; and constantly needs Allah's guidance and forgiveness. Since everyone is the same in the eyes of God, all men and women are equal. Every individual is endowed with free will and has the choice to do good or bad. Everyone is ultimately individually accountable to God for his or her actions and will be judged after death.

This implies our existence does not end with death; there is life after death of reward and punishment. We should thus behave in this life in such a manner that we may not suffer in life after death. And, this applies not just to individuals but society as a whole which should follow the path of justice and equity.

The Muslim conception of God is often criticized by Westerners as austere and severe. It is certainly true Islam has no notion of 'God the Father' and specifically proscribes the idea of 'God incarnate'. But such comments fail to capture how ordinary Muslims experience and understand the idea of God. For a Muslim, the Infinite – while awesome and all-powerful – is also an ever-present reality, as witnessed by the innumerable idioms of Muslim daily speech that invoke and refer to Allah. Travelers to the Middle East frequently encounter the phrase *Alhumdu lil Allah*: 'Praise be to

Why I am a Muslim

The strangest question I have ever been asked is: why are you Muslim? I find the question strange because I have never thought of a reason. My 'Muslimness' comes naturally to me; no other alternative has ever crossed my mind. I am Muslim because the only logical explanation of all the wonder in the universe and in ourselves is that a Creator exists. Every breath I take is a mercy from that Creator. To deny God, I would be denying myself and my life. Indeed, I see God's miracles everywhere, I can not but love, worship and obey Him. Through God's commands, revealed in the Qur'an and the examples of the Prophet Muhammad, I know exactly how to live my life. I am free to choose between peace and happiness by becoming a part of God's greater design, and the nightmare of rejecting my Creator's guidance. I am Muslim because I choose to be logical and far-sighted. I see the logic of Islam and am far-sighted enough to plan for the eternity that God has offered. ∎

Marwa El-Naggar, an Egyptian woman in her 20s.

Allah'. Indeed, Arabs never seem to tire of uttering this and other similar phrases.

They affirm the Muslim belief that God is nearer to a person than their jugular vein, a perceptible presence all-knowing and all-seeing, constantly aware of each individual, their thoughts, motivations and deeds. For Muslims, the essence of religion is human effort to remain conscious of God's presence. And that is exactly what most pious Muslims strive to do.

The second part of the *shahadah*, the declaration that Prophet Muhammad is the Messenger of God, signifies God is not only present in an abstract sense but is actually known through revelation. Revelation, the self-declaration of God to human society through the medium of human prophets makes religion an historic presence in human society. For Muslims, the Qur'an is the direct word of God, an enduring record of the specific Revelation made to the Prophet between the years 610 and 633AD. But the Qur'an is not the only instance of revelation nor is Prophet Muhammad the only Prophet acknowledged by Islam. The Qur'an specifically names 25 Prophets, including Abraham (Ibrahim in the Qur'an), Moses (Musa) and Jesus (Isa) and many others familiar from the Bible. Christians and Jews are 'the People of the Book' and both the Old and the New Testaments are regarded by Islam as revealed – although corrupted – texts. But the Qur'an also refers to many more unnamed Prophets and states no society has been without a messenger; Muslims are required to give equal respect to all Prophets.

Prophets are recipients of specific divine guidance on how to live. Conceptually, prophethood means knowledge of God is not only innate in human nature but also the foundation of human history. The first Prophet according to Islam was Adam, the first human. Furthermore, all prophets brought the same basic message of Islam, recognition and acceptance of God. While the specifics of particular revelations, the rules and precepts of observance and living, may differ and human society may deviate from or distort the message of divine guidance, for Islam at core the moral challenge of living a good life in consciousness of God is the same for all peoples whatever their religious affiliation. What distinguishes Prophet Muhammad is that he is considered the last, or Seal of the Prophets, the revelation he received being a complete and enduring form of God's message for all humanity.

Thus, the basic articles of faith in Islam are three:
- Belief in the Unity of God;
- Belief in the Prophethood of Prophet Muhammad and the Message of guidance he received;
- Belief in the life after death and accountability on the Day of Judgment.

The Pillars

The *shahadah* is considered as the first 'pillar' of Islam. It is used in the *azan* or call to prayer. Every day, in every Muslim society, the believers are ushered to the mosque with these words:

> **God is the Most Great.**
> **I bear witness that there is no god but God.**
> **I bear witness that Muhammad is the messenger of God.**
> **Come to prayer.**
> **Come to success.**
> **God is the Most Great.**
> **There is no god but God.**

Prayer, or *salat*, is the second pillar of Islam. Muslims are required to pray five times a day; wherever possible in congregation. But prayer is always an individual act of worship, a way of acquiring God consciousness in one's daily life. The midday prayer on Friday is a compulsory congregational prayer, bringing the entire neighborhood together for worship and social interaction. People who may be negligent of their daily prayers make a special effort to attend the Friday prayers. Prayer consists of recitation of verses from the Qur'an within a ritual pattern of movements established by the Prophet Muhammad. In congregational prayers worshippers stand in straight lines facing the direction of Mecca and are led by an *Imam*. Anyone can be an Imam and lead a prayer but it helps if they have a rudimentary of knowledge of Islam!

The third pillar of Islam is fasting during the month of Ramadan. Fasting is a spiritual and physical discipline, a way of learning self-control and teaching an appreciation of the trials and tribulations of hunger. Ramadan, the 9th month of the Muslim year, is known as the blessed month. It was in this month Prophet Muhammad received his first revelation. During Ramadan Muslims are required to make extra efforts to spread love, peace, harmony and good will. As the Muslim year is a based on a lunar calendar, Ramadan moves through the seasons and the months of calendars based on the Solar year, beginning approximately 11 days earlier each year. During Ramadan, special but voluntary evening prayers – known as *tarawih* – are held where, over the course of the month, the whole of the Qur'an is read. During these prayers, the Imam has to be a *hafiz* – someone who has memorized the Qur'an by heart. Each day's fast begins just before dawn and ends at sunset; during the fast it is forbidden to eat, drink, smoke or have sex. People who are sick, young children, the very old and those who are traveling, menstruating and pregnant women are exempt from fasting. The end of the month of Ramadan is marked by the festival of Eid al-Fitr, during which the entire community comes together for a large, thanks-giving, congregational prayer.

Ramadan makes a marked change in daily routine and in some countries introduces a new way of life. In

Saudi Arabia and much of the Arabian peninsula, for example, people tend to sleep most of the day and work during the night: shops are closed between 11.00 am and 5.00 pm, the streets are deserted, and come back to life after sunset. While people are supposed to eat less during Ramadan, breaking the fast is an occasion for celebration and may lead to eating rather more than usual.

Zakat, often called the 'poor due' or 'religious tax', is the fourth pillar of Islam. The word *zakah* means to purify; the purification of one's income by giving a proportion to the poor and the needy and for general public welfare is a religious duty for every Muslim. *Zakat* is normally given annually – traditionally at the end of Ramadan – and has to be at least 2.5 per cent of annual income or 'appropriated wealth'. 'Appropriated wealth' excludes debts and liabilities, household effects (except jewelry) required for living; and land, buildings, and capital materials used in or for production; but includes almost everything by which one makes a profit. No-one is exempt from *zakat*: even the dead have *zakat* deducted from their estate before inheritance and legacies are disbursed.

Zakat can be collected by social or welfare organizations on behalf of the community or by the State itself. But it can only be spent for certain specified purposes including to assist the poor, the homeless, the bankrupt, the needy, for education or medical treatment for those who cannot afford to pay and public works that enhance the general welfare of a community. Nowadays, many Muslim countries like Pakistan, Malaysia and Iran have state institutions that collect and distribute *zakat*. In Britain and America, during the last two decades, numerous non-governmental organizations – with names like 'Islamic Relief', 'Muslim Aid' and 'Muslim Hands' – have emerged for collecting and distributing *zakat* funds to refugees, victims of war and natural disasters.

The fifth and final pillar of Islam is hajj – the

The Islamic Year

Month	Festival
Muharram	Shia Muslims celebrate the martyrdom of Imam Hussain. The 10th is Ashura, a voluntary day of fasting.
Safar	
Rabi al-Awal	The 12th is Eid Milad un-Nabi, or the birthday of the Prophet Muhammad
Rabi al-Thani	
Jumada al-Ula	
Jumada al-Thani	
Rajab	The 27th is Lalat-ul Miraj, or the Night of the Miraj, the Prophet's Ascension to Heaven
Shaban	
Ramadan	The month of obligatory fasting. The 27th is the 'Night of the Power', the celebration of the first revelation to the Prophet Muhammad
Shawwal	The 1st is Eid al-Fitr, the celebration of the end of the Ramadan fast.
Dhu al-Qadah	
Dhul Hijjah	The month of the hajj, which occurs during the 9th and 12th days. The 9th is the Day of Arafat; and the 10th Eid al-Adha, when Muslims all over the world join the pilgrims in celebrating the ethical and humanitarian concerns of Islam. ■

pilgrimage to Mecca. Every Muslim who is physically able and can afford to undertake the journey is required to perform the hajj at least once in their life-time. It is considered the supreme spiritual experience of a Muslim's life, a journey undertaken for individual self-renewal inspired by piety and devotion to God. It is performed during the month of Dhul Hijjah, two months after Ramadan; and like Ramadan it moves through the solar year covering the four seasons during a 30-year period. It falls on the 9th, 10th, 11th and 12th days of the month and like prayer follows a pattern established by Prophet Muhammad.

The word 'hajj' means effort – and the hajj requires a great deal of physical and mental effort. The pilgrims – on average over two million each year – travel in a vast company and are required to perform certain rituals at prescribed times. They begin by discarding their normal attire and entering the state of *ihram*. For men, the *ihram* consists of two simple, unsewn, white sheets of cloth (frequently two large towels); women wear plain, usually white, loose, full-length dress with a head-scarf. Once in *ihram*, the pilgrims have to follow strict rules of conduct: they cannot do anything dishonest or arrogant, show aggression or use abusive words, or shout at anyone in anger. They must show respect towards nature: even an insect should not be harmed. They cannot cut their hair or fingernails and must abstain from sex. Indeed, all material pleasures have to be abandoned; even the use of scented soap is not allowed.

After donning *ihram*, the pilgrims go straight to the Sacred Mosque in Mecca, the location of the *Ka'aba*, the stone shrine covered with a black cloth. For Muslims, it is the prime focus of Islam: they turn towards the *Ka'aba* when they pray; metaphorically, it symbolizes the unity and common sense of purpose and direction in life. The pilgrims walk round the *Ka'aba* seven times, a ritual known as the *tawaf*. Then, they perform the ritual of Sai, running between the two small hills of Safa and Marwah. This ritual commemorates the desperate search for water of Hagar, the wife of Prophet Abraham. Abandoned thirst-stricken in the heat and desolation near the *Ka'aba* along with her infant son, Ishmael, Hagar ran seven times up and down the hills in search of water. Then, the tradition has it, the spring of Zamzam gushed forth. The pilgrims re-enact this scene and end the ritual by drinking Zamzam water. Nowadays the entire Sai area is covered with a splendid structure and air-conditioned. Both the Sai and Zamzam are within the area of the Sacred Mosque. Spiritually, this ritual signifies the soul's desperate search for meaning and that which gives it true life.

The *tawaf* and Sai rituals comprise the 'lesser pilgrimage' or *umra* – which can be performed at any time during the year. The hajj requires additional rituals. On the 8th of Dhul Hijjah, the pilgrims travel to spend the night at nearby Muna. The 9th is the main day when the pilgrims descend to the plains of Arafat. Here, the entire congregation of some two million people offers the noon prayer as a single unit. After the collective prayer, they stand together under the burning sun to pray individually for forgiveness. The prayer and the ritual of standing is the essence of hajj. It is here that pilgrims experience an unparalleled sense of a brotherhood and sisterhood; but their overriding experience is personal: 'It is I and my Lord; and the noblest hours of my life.'

At the end of the Day of Arafat pilgrims make a dash to Muzdalifah, an open plain sheltered by parched hills between Arafat and Muna. Here they spend a night under the open sky. The next day they return to Muna, staying for three days during which they perform the ritual of Stoning, throwing three pebbles at each of the three stone pillars symbolizing the Devil. Tradition has it the Devil tried to tempt Prophet Abraham and his family at these spots. Remembering the incident, the pilgrims promise to cast out their own devil within. Finally, the pilgrims take off their ihram, have a bath, sacrifice an animal for the benefit of the poor (although some simply give money to charity) and close the hajj with celebration. Muslims throughout the world join the pilgrims in celebration of Eid al-Adha, the feast of sacrifice.

Until quite recently, the environment of hajj –

Mecca, the surrounding areas of Muna, Muzdalifah and Arafat – had remained largely unchanged from the times of the Prophet. But from 1970s onwards the entire region was extensively re-developed. Virtually all the historic cultural property was destroyed – even the hills, so steeped in history, were flattened. So, despite its sacred nature, and its central place in Muslim tradition, the city of Mecca appears to have no relation to Islamic history. It resembles Houston!

Tradition

The hajj provides a good example of Islam's emphasis on tradition. It invokes the historical narratives of Prophet Abraham, the founder of the monotheistic faiths, to whom Islam traces its origins. Like all religions, Islam aspires to maintain continuity with its original vision. Tradition is the soil from which the tree of Islam takes its nourishment to grow and flower. As a Persian proverb says, 'as long as the roots of the plant are in the water there is still hope'. For Muslims, tradition is like water – something that sustains and rejuvenates them. Pious Muslims everywhere thus strive to live within the traditions of Islam.

Islamic tradition was shaped in the process by which the practice of Prophet Muhammad came to be accepted as normative for the Muslim community. The words and actions of the Prophet became oral and written reports and came to be known as Traditions, which became a major branch of study soon after the Prophet's death. The reports were meticulously collected, critiqued and rejected or accepted as authentic; and became the basis for shaping Muslim values. These records are known as the *sunnah*; literally, the example of the Prophet. The sayings are referred to as *hadith*. Together, *sunnah* and *hadith* constitute the Traditions. These Traditions have been used in a variety of ways by the Muslim community, from law and scholarship to popular sayings, parables and homilies that sprinkle ordinary discussion.

The Traditions have kept the example and personality of the Prophet alive in Muslim consciousness. They provide Muslims with a rounded sense of a real human being and how he interacted with his followers. What is familiar to Muslims from reading *hadith* is a person of profound spirituality and humility with unfailing compassion and concern for fellow human beings. A man with a gentle sense of humor who is tolerant, forgiving and sympathetic of the failings and foibles of his fellow citizens, concerned for the dignity of each individual and utterly committed to improving the material as well as the spiritual condition of their lives.

The Traditions became the basis for the elaboration of Islamic legal principles. As noted, the Qur'an itself contains very few specific legal injunctions. Therefore from the outset both the Qur'an and how the Prophet determined matters, especially in his role as leader of the community, became a basis for developing Islamic Law, or *sharia*. Subsequent rulers of the Muslim community would request opinions from those learned in the Traditions to help them determine policy, a process in which politics, vested interests and differences of outlook played their part. Literally, the word sharia means 'the path or the road leading to water'. In its religious use, it has come to mean 'the highway of good life': that is, religious values expressed in concrete terms to shape and direct the lives of believers. In this way, the sharia is the path not only leading to

Authentic *hadith* collections

There are six collections of *hadith* regarded as most authoritative, often called canonical. These are: *Sahih Bukhari*, collected by Muhammad bin Ismail often called Imam Bukhari; the *Sahih Muslim*, of Muslim bin al-Hajjaj; the *Sunan Abu Dawud*, of Sulaiman bin Ash'ath, known as Abu Dawud; *the Sunan Ibn Majah* of Muhammad bin Yazid ; the *Jami' At-Tirmidhi* of Muhammad bin Isa; and the *Sunan An-Nasa'i* of Ahmad bin Shu'aib. All of these collectors of *hadith* lived and died between the 8th and 9th centuries. ■

God; but the path shown by God through the Qur'an and the example of the Traditions of the Prophet. Collectively, the sharia provides a legal framework for family relations, crime and punishment, inheritance, trade and commerce, the organization and operation of communal affairs and relations between communities and states.

The Qur'an and the Traditions of the Prophet are not the only source of Islamic Law. Over the years, the custom and practice of early Muslim communities also became an integral part of the sharia. Legal consensus (*ijma*) of classical jurists acquired the force of sharia law and became binding on later communities. Slowly, a huge body of traditional jurisprudence, known as *fiqh*, became indistinguishable from the original sharia. *Fiqh* was largely a product of human efforts to understand and comprehend the message of the Qur'an and the Traditions. It evolved on the basis of the Islamic concept of *ijtihad* or systematic original thinking. But during the 14th century, religious scholars closed 'the gates of *ijtihad*' – and both sharia and *fiqh* became trapped in the traditions of the early Muslim communities. Contemporary Islam therefore tries systematically to replicate the customs and tradition of the classical period. How this system operates today is examined in chapter 8.

Fiqh, however, is not a monolithic body of traditional jurisprudence. Right from the beginning, there were strong differences of opinion between the classical jurists leading to five distinct Schools of Thought – or *madhabs* – named after the most eminent jurists of the period: Imam Malik, Imam Shafi'i, Imam Abu Hanafi, Imam Ahmad ibn Hanbali and Imam Jafar al-Sadiq.

The Maliki School, which was based in Medina, is the oldest and most deeply immersed in Arab traditions. It is now dominant in most countries of Muslim Africa. But the largest and most important School of the classical period is the Shafi'i which evolved in

Baghdad, the capital of the Abbasid Caliphate (652-1258). More sophisticated than the austere Maliki tradition, it gave more emphasis to free will and *ijma*, or consensus, of the community. The Hanafi School, considered to be more rationalist, developed as a reaction against the narrow traditionalism of Maliki Arabs. Imam Hanafi relied more on legal reasoning and precedents than on *hadith* in developing his thought. He also developed court procedures and rules of evidence and cautioned against extreme punishments. The Hanafi School is followed in Egypt, Turkey and much of Southeast Asia. The Hanbali is undoubtedly the most puritanical of all Schools of Thought. Imam Hanbali rejected the use of legal reasoning as well as *ijma*, and insisted that sharia be based exclusively on literal interpretation of the Qur'an. Saudi Arabia is the only Muslim country where the Hanbali creed is the state religion. The Jafari School, dominant largely in Iran and Iraq, is followed principally by Shi'a Muslims. Imam Jafar believed only direct descendents of the Prophet Muhammad have the right to interpret the sharia.

The overall emphasis of *fiqh* is on worldly life. But the classical period also saw the parallel evolution of a totally different tradition focused on the mystical content of the Qur'an and Traditions of the Prophet. The mystical tradition of Islam is called *Sufism* and is based on the concept of *tariqah*, the path of union with God. The word *Sufi* comes from the Arabic *suf* meaning wool; it refers to the undyed wool garments that early mystics of Islam, eschewing luxuries of dress and shelter and preferring an ascetic life of simplicity and poverty, used to wear. An alternative name for Sufism, used mostly in Muslim circles, is *tasawwuf*, again from the same root word, it denotes 'the practice of wearing the woolen robe' and hence the act of devoting oneself to mystical life. One of the first Sufis was the great women saint Rabia Basri, who developed the doctrine of 'disinterested love of God' which became both the basic motif of her life and a central tenet of Sufism.

In general, Sufis work to overcome the appetites and desires of the human body and thus purify the heart in preparation for union with God. The final goal is to become so close to God that human consciousness becomes totally absorbed in consciousness of God. This final state is known as *fana*: the annihilation of one's self and its dissolution in the love of God. In Islamic history, the most celebrated Sufi to achieve this goal is the Persian mystic, al-Hallaj, who in a state of *fana* declared: 'I am Truth'. Another central tenet of Sufism is the notion of Wahdat al-wajud, or 'unity of all being', associated with the name of the great Andalusian Sufi, Muhyi al-Din ibn Arabi. He frequently used a prayer which begins: 'Enter me, O Lord, into the deep of the Ocean of Thine Infinite Oneness'. Within Sufi mysticism, as in *fiqh*, there are different interpretations and approaches. There is devotional mysticism as well as intellectual and philosophical mysticism. Authority in Sufism belongs to the Sheikh, often considered the Perfect Master, who guides his followers in their mystical quest. There are many Sufi Orders, each with its own specific esoteric practices, each tracing its lineage to a great Sufi of the classical age with whose name the order is normally associated. The chain of transmission, or the *silsilah*, connects the Sufi masters of the present day with the grand masters and then to the Prophet Muhammad himself in a master-to-master line. Amongst the well-known Sufi Orders are the *Qadiriyyah*, founded by the Indian Sufi Abd al-Qadir Jilani, the *Chishti* Order founded by Abd al-Qadir's contemporary Muin ad-Din Chishti, the *Shadhiliyyah* order established by the North African Sufi Abu-Hasan ash-Shadhili and the *Maluvi* order associated by the great Persian/Turkish mystical poet, Jalal al-Din Rumi.

Throughout its history, Sufism has been in simmering conflict with orthodox, *fiqh*-based, Islam.

Sometimes, this conflict has boiled over: the orthodox had al-Hallaj executed for uttering and ascribing a central attribute of God – Truth – to himself.

Worldview

The religion and tradition of Islam, as well as its culture and civilization, are connected by the worldview of Islam. This worldview is shaped by a set of ideas, the concepts set forth in the Qur'an, the Traditions of the Prophet and embedded in their teaching and examples. It is these religious concepts and their associated norms and values that shaped the civilization of Islam in history and provide a coherent outlook across its diversity. Indeed, it is the understanding, interpretation, the actual and potential meaning given to these concepts, past and present, that gives Islamic civilization its particular character.

The fundamental concept of the Islamic worldview is *tawhid*, normally translated as 'the unity of God'. Islam is concerned not just with belief in one God but also the oneness of God and hence the unity of His creation. So, by extension this signifies the unity of humankind and the unity of people and nature. *Tawhid* is the significance behind that most familiar of Muslim expressions: *Allahu Akbar*, God is Great. It means nothing except God is eternal; everything other than God is limited and finite and belongs to God alone. Within this all-embracing unity creation is a trust from God, and men and women – equal in the sight of God whatever their color or creed – are *khalifah* or trustees of God. Therefore, human beings are not the absolute owner of existence, neither their own, that of other creatures nor the natural environment. People are temporary and transient users of this trust, *amanah*, therefore each individual and each community are responsible and accountable for how this trust is used. A steward or trustee should husband and nurture the resources entrusted to them and ensure they are handed to future users, subsequent generations, in the best possible condition. The idea of *khalifah* establishes humankind's place in the order of creation. It also sees that place as a relationship in time, within the succession of history, as well as in relation to what is beyond time, the return of each individual to God for judgment in the Hereafter.

Tawhid, or the unity of the Creator, gives significance and order to creation. Implicit in the created order are signs, known in Arabic as *ayah*, that help humanity to understand His creation. The *ayahs* of the Creator can be understood, and the responsibility of trusteeship fulfilled, through three other fundamental Islamic concepts: *ilm* (knowledge), *adl* (distributive social justice) and *ijtihad* (sustained intellectual reasoning). The thought and action of the *khalifah* are based not on blind faith but on knowledge and sustained intellectual effort; and the major function of all the ideas and actions of the trustee are to promote all-round justice.

Ilm, or knowledge, is a cardinal concept of Islam. Almost one third of the Qur'an is devoted to extolling the virtues of knowledge. Prophet Muhammad consistently urged it on his followers: 'seek knowledge from the cradle to the grave'; 'to spend more time in learning is better than spending more time in prayer'; 'knowledge is like the lost camel of a Muslim, take hold of it whenever you come across it', he is reported to have said. Not surprisingly the pursuit of knowledge and learning is considered to be the sacred duty of all Muslims, females as well as males. *Ijtihad* relates specifically to knowledge in religious matters. It functions to focus attention on the challenge of changing circumstances and the struggle to comprehend the meaning of religion in application to contemporary life.

Like *ilm*, *adl* too is a consistent theme running through the Qur'an, the sayings of the Prophet and reverberating in Muslim discourses throughout history. Its meaning as distributive justice is most clearly seen in one of the five pillars of Islam: *zakat*, whose

Monotheistic faiths

Islam regards itself as a continuation of Judaism and Christianity. The three monotheistic faiths share common threads. The Christian Bible includes the Judaic Old Testament in addition to the teachings of Jesus. The Qur'an refers to events in both the Old and New Testaments in addition to the prophetic career of Prophet Muhammad.

All three faiths share a common ancestor in Abraham, or Ibrahim. Details of his prophetic career are central to the most basic aspects of Muslim worship, from turning to the *Ka'aba* when they pray to the details of performing the hajj, the pilgrimage to Mecca.

While the New Testament builds upon the Old Testament, Christianity and Judaism are distinctly different faiths each with their own traditions of worship and practice. The same is true of Islam. The Qur'an presents the story of Prophet Adam and his wife, Hawa in Muslim tradition. But the detail and import are distinct. In the Qur'anic story both Adam and Eve were tempted, both erred equally, repented and both were forgiven. So for Muslims all human beings, male and female, begin life sinless, equally capable of error and reform.

One chapter of the Qur'an is entitled Mariam, named for Mary the mother of Jesus (Isa). Muslims accept the virgin birth of Jesus, his prophetic mission and crucifixion, but not his death on the cross or resurrection. And while Jesus, like all Prophets, is honored by Muslims he is considered human and not divine.

The encounter between Moses (Musa) and Pharaoh also features in the Qur'an. Pharaoh is a symbol of the arrogance, corruption and tyranny of earthly power. The decay and downfall of Empires is a recurrent Qur'anic theme used to emphasize human potential for error by turning away from God consciousness.

Similar narratives, differently told and interpreted, link Islam, Christianity and Judaism. But a more significant and neglected point is that these shared narratives point to common moral and ethical values and perceptions that stand just behind the different language of explication and interpretation of the three monotheistic faiths. ∎

function is providing a constant supply of funds for the needy. But there are a host of other concepts associated with *adl*. *Riba* is specifically the prohibition of interest but conceptually it is a powerful general principle working against the accumulation of superfluous riches in the hands of a few by providing the means and opportunity for those in need to better their circumstances. *Mudaraba*, for example, means sharing and participation founded on the proposition that all human activity includes risk; what is unavoidable and common to all should be equitably shared by all.

Furthermore, Islamic rules of inheritance – whose calculation gave rise to algebra – require that one's wealth should be apportioned in fixed proportions among one's immediate family members and then distributed amongst a broader range of relatives to ensure that wealth and resources are not concentrated in fewer and fewer hands.

Distributive justice

Distributive justice not only operates to secure the circulation of resources through society it seeks to ensure human dignity by creating the means and opportunity for achieving self-reliance. The pursuit of justice may require one to engage in jihad or righteous struggle to bring forth justice. Jihad begins with oneself; indeed, morally transcending the limitations of one's human failings and frailty is its highest form. Much of Sufism is devoted to personal jihad – the suppression of one's ego. Jihad extends to seeking justice with one's wealth, economic jihad, and one's knowledge, intellectual jihad. The final stage of jihad is armed struggle of the Muslim community as a whole against an unjust ruler. We will consider how this concept operates in today's world in chapter 8.

Both *adl* and *ilm* are to be sought on the basis of *ijma* (consensus), *shura* (consultation) and *istislah* (public interest). The Islamic worldview is deeply consensus-orientated: it seeks to bring the Muslim community together on the basis of general, wide ranging agreements. How a community should determine and organize itself to perform its tasks and fulfill its purpose as the trustee of God is delineated in the concept of *shura*. *Shura* is a procedure of consultation in which all members of the community have the right to participate and be heard. It also means decisions arrived at by consensus, the participatory engagement of citizens should result in their informed consent and acceptance of collective decisions. *Shura* provides an operative model for putting mutual responsibility into action.

The objective of communal decision-making is *istislah*, the public interest, the common good. Consultation and debate clearly require the freedom to express opinions, to criticize and question, to call officials to account. It is a prerequisite of the familiar phrase that sums up the purpose and defining character of the Muslim community: Islam: promoting what is right and forbidding what is wrong. What is right and wholesome, what promotes knowledge and justice, public interest and consensus, is considered *halal* (praiseworthy); outside this framework, where lies dissension, injustice and ignorance, and hence danger, is the *haram* (blameworthy) territory. *Halal* and *haram* are the axes upon which all concepts and elements of the Islamic worldview are assessed and operate. Thus halal food, now a common feature in Western societies is not merely a method of slaughtering meat. It should mean an entire process from production of food by sensitive ecologically sound methods through a chain of processing and marketing to consumption that is beneficial to the environment, human health and provides just returns to those employed at each stage of the process.

The Islamic term for community is *ummah*, specifically it identifies the global community of believers, Muslims, those who are faithful to the religion, Tradition and the worldview of Islam. All Muslims wherever they live, whether in majority states or as minority communities, are constituent parts of and belong to the *ummah*. The *ummah*, as Prophet Muhammad said, is like a human body: if one part hurts the whole body feels the pain. 'But one is not born into it by blind chance; one is elected and joins

Major world religions

Islam is considered the fastest growing religion in the world. Muslims consititute a fifth of humanity. Most are under 25.

TOTAL WORLD POPULATION
6.1 billion
MAJOR RELIGIONS
Christianity 2 billion
Islam 1.3 billion
Hinduism 900 million
Buddhism 360 million

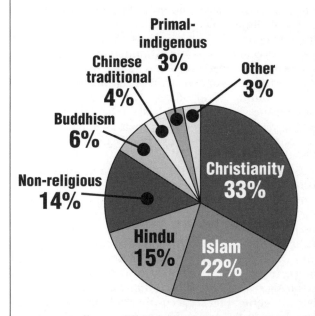

- Around 85 per cent of Muslims belong to the majority Sunni sect. The minority Shi'a Muslims are concentrated in Iran and Iraq.
- Less than 20 per cent of Muslims are Arabs. Almost half of the world's Muslims live in South and Southeast Asia.

Statistical, Economic and Social Research and Training Center for Islamic Countries (SESRTCIC), Ankara, Turkey, *National Geographic*, January 2002.

it as a rational being. The *ummah* is not a community-by-nature, but a community-by-decision, a "society"'.[1] The *ummah* constantly seeks *islah*, meaning reform or setting right, the ongoing search for practical and sustainable ways to improve the condition of human life, individually and for the community as a whole. *Islah* is a reformative rather than revolutionary concept. Each individual as well as human society is potentially perfectible, but also prone to error, to being far from perfect. Reform is, therefore, a continual necessity that must take account of actual circumstances and real human needs. Setting things right requires continuous amendment by increments that work to move individuals and society nearer to achieving the enduring values, the moral and ethical percepts of Islam.

All of these concepts are part of a unity, they are interrelated and place emphasis on developing a way of thinking and operating grounded in holistic understanding. The objective is to seek balance and moderation with one concept tempering and affecting the understanding of all others. The concept of *tawhid*, oneness or wholeness, emphasizes the necessity of not taking particular elements or texts in isolation, or out of context. It is in this sense that Islam is regarded by Muslims as the Middle Way.

Collectively, the religion, tradition and worldview of Islam constitute the *din*: Islam's description of itself. The term *din* translates as an entire way of life for an individual as a member of society with the complementary meaning of a way of life for a society of individuals. It also contains the idea that religion, tradition and worldview shapes the way of knowing, being and doing of any society, that they provide the bedrock, the civilizing conscience of both individual and society. In its most general sense, according to Islam, all societies, whether Muslim or not, have a *din*, a civilizational core of principles from which its characteristic way of life and attitudes to life are derived. Explicitly, Islam as religion and worldview is an understanding of what it is to be human and the nature and organization of human existence. The term *din* emphasizes that all that exists shares a basic unity and partakes of a common sacredness, all is interconnected. From the perspective of Islam nothing is or can be entirely secular, in the sense of solely of this present world.

1 R al-Faruqi, *Tawheed: Its Implication for Thought and Life* (International Institute of Islamic Thought, Washington, 1982, p 139).

3 The Rightly Guided Caliphs

After the Prophet Muhammad, no-one could inherit the mantle of prophethood. But his four closest companions who took over the leadership of the Muslim community came to be known as al-Khulafa ar rashidun, or the 'Rightly Guided Caliphs'. The term 'Rightly Guided' signifies their actions are accepted by all Muslims as closest to the Prophet's example. After him, their words and actions are the most authoritative source on Muslim behavior.

THE DEATH OF the Prophet in 632 AD made the question of who should lead the Muslim community a matter of urgent discussion and debate. As usual, people gathered at the Prophet's Mosque in Medina. A number of prominent persons suggested that Abu Bakr, the closest associate and friend of Prophet Muhammad, should be asked to take over the political leadership of the community. The matter was settled by the unanimous election of Abu Bakr.

Abu Bakr

The speech Abu Bakr made on his election as the First Caliph of Islam has reverberated as an ideal in Muslim consciousness ever since: 'O people, I have been chosen by you as your leader, although I am no better than any one of you. If I do good, give me your support. If I do any wrong, set me right... The weak among you are the powerful in my eyes, as long as I do not get them their dues. The powerful among you are weak in my eyes, as long as I do not take away from them what is due to others... Obey me as long as I obey Allah and His messenger. If I disobey Allah and His messenger, you are free to disobey me.'

Abu Bakr was, like the Prophet, a merchant from Mecca. After his election he continued to go to the market to trade cloth. He was assured by Umar, soon to be his successor, that it was no longer necessary for him to pursue his trade and that the public treasury would provide him with a 'middling pension.' His stipend included one garment for winter, one for summer, and a daily allowance of lamb for food.

Two years younger than the Prophet, Abu Bakr served as Caliph or leader for just over two years; he died in 634. He had to deal with the many groups across Arabia who regarded their allegiance as given personally to Prophet Muhammad. He moved swiftly to reassert unity, seeking to make the bonds of common religion predominate over kinship. This included tackling economic revolts by groups who refused to pay *zakat*. The second aspect of his caliphate was expansion beyond Arabia. Expeditions were launched both to Syria and Palestine, then part of the Byzantine Empire, and Iraq, part of the Persian Empire. In 634 a Byzantine (Eastern Roman Empire) Christian force was defeated at the Battle of Ajnadain, 30 miles south west of Jerusalem, the remnant of their army falling back on the heavily fortified city. Most of the Palestinian cities submitted to the Muslim forces. On the Persian front inroads had been made into Iraq and an as yet inconclusive campaign against Persian forces was under way.

In 634 the ailing Abu Bakr consulted with senior Companions of the Prophet and nominated Umar ibn al-Khattab to be his successor. Their approval was readily granted and Umar became the Second Caliph of Islam.

Umar

Umar, Caliph from 634-44, was the first to adopt the title of Amir al-Mu'minin, Commander of the Faithful, which was retained by all later Caliphs. At the time of his accession Muslim forces were laying siege to Damascus, which surrendered in 635. In 637/8 Jerusalem was on the point of surrender, but its citizens insisted they would capitulate only to the Caliph himself. Umar traveled from Medina and the

Jerusalemites were amazed to see their new ruler arrive barefoot, poorly dressed, after a journey on which he had taken turns riding his camel with the one servant who accompanied him. Umar proclaimed that those who submitted to Muslim rule would have their lives, property and places of worship protected. This became the accepted precedent that laid the foundation for the heterodox nature of the new empire. Muslim forces were also engaged in Iraq. By 640 the campaign against the Persians concluded with the collapse of the Sassanid dynasty, most of their territory coming under Muslim rule. The coastal cities of Syria and Palestine, supported by forces from Alexandria in Egypt, were taken the following year. The victorious Muslim commander, Amr ibn al-As, then moved on to invade Egypt which was conquered by 642.

This vast territory needed a system of administration. Umar was largely responsible for establishing the form and character of this system. He introduced a highly developed fiscal system in which the public treasury raised revenue through personal and property taxation. The *kharaj* was a tax calculated according to the productivity of the land; the *jizya*, a personal tax paid by non-Muslims. During Umar's time Muslim forces were not permitted to become landowners in the newly acquired territory. Muslims, of course, were required to pay *zakat*. This distinction is the basis of what later came to be known as the *dhimmi* status, from *ahl ad dhimmah*, the category of 'protected people'. It is a matter of considerable controversy between Muslim and non-Muslim commentators. The controversy is whether non-Muslims were second-class citizens. Muslim scholars argued that as non-Muslims were exempt from military service, the *jizya* was largely a tax in lieu of military service. At the outset the various *dhimmi* communities were granted a degree of autonomy and their religious leadership was responsible for the collection and payment of their taxes to the administration.

Umar standardized the disbursement of state income. The customary practice of dividing the spoils was replaced by a *diwan* or registration of the Arab Muslims who were paid a proportionate pension, even down to slaves and children. He thus established that all citizens had a claim on the resources of the State. That those in need, whether Muslim or non-Muslim, had a right to assistance by state funds was a basic Qur'anic proposition. He organized the territory into a series of provinces and appointed a Governor for each. Living a simple even austere life himself, Umar was concerned at the potential consequences for Muslim forces occupying the wealthy and grandiose cities of the Middle East.

In 637, after his commanders sacked the Persian capital, Ctesiphon on the banks of the Tigris, some 20 miles southeast of where Baghdad would be founded in 763, he ordered a military camp to be made outside the town. Kufa, the site of this camp, developed into a city. It became famous as a center for the study of Arabic grammar and the distinctive geometric script of writing Arabic known as *Kufic* derives its name from this new city. Establishing cities became a pattern. When Muslim forces conquered Egypt in 641-2 they founded the city of Fustat, which continued to be the capital until 973 when it moved to Cairo (founded in 969). Muslim territorial advance proceeded with the building of new cities; Muslim civilization was an urban culture, a culture of the *medina*, the generic term for a city.

In 644 Umar was murdered by Feroz Abu Lu'Lu'ah, a disgruntled Persian servant of the Governor of Basra. The servant's complaint over taxation had been dismissed and in retaliation he stabbed Umar while he was gathering worshippers for morning prayers in the mosque of Medina. Fatally wounded, Umar appointed an Electoral Council of seven Companions of the Prophet to choose his successor. He ordered the Council to consult the chiefs of all the clans as well as prominent members of the Medina community and reach a decision within three days. The Council chose Othman bin Affan, then nearly 70 years old.

Othman

Othman had been doubly Prophet Muhammad's son in law. He had married Ruqaiya and after her death Umm Kulthum; neither daughter survived the Prophet. It is during the 12 years of Othman's Caliphate that tensions within the Muslim community came to the fore, organized along principles that over time came to identify different schools of thought, different factions and trends within the Islamic community.

Territorial expansion was consolidated during Othman's Caliphate. Attempts by Byzantium to recapture Egypt were repulsed. Byzantine power however still continued to pose a threat because of its sea-power. In response a Muslim navy, founded in 649, was developed. The shipyards of Egypt and Syria were operated in a collaborative effort between the Muslim forces and the indigenous Christian seamen. In the year of its founding a naval attack was launched on Cyprus. In 653 Cyprus was again attacked and Rhodes was also captured. In 655 the Byzantine navy suffered a disastrous defeat at the hands of Muslim sea-power. With Egypt secure, advances were made further across North Africa. In the east, around 650, Muslim forces pressed forward into Khursan, the easternmost region of the Persian Empire, advancing into what is today Afghanistan.

Othman's single greatest achievement was the production of an authorized written Qur'an, completed by 652. But he was accused of nepotism in appointing members of his own clan as provincial governors and to key administrative posts. While Othman himself led a simple life there was growing concern the enormous riches generated by conquest were having a

corrupting effect on the administration. Some argued that the riches gathered should all be spent on charity. There was resentment at the despotism of the Umayyad officials, members of the aristocratic Umayya clan of Mecca, to which Othman himself belonged. The widely dispersed armies became a seedbed of discontent and sedition. There were revolts in Kufa, Basra and Fustat. Muhammad, son of the first Caliph Abu Bakr, led a group of insurgents from Egypt and besieged the Caliph in his house in Medina. Breaking into the house they murdered Othman as he sat reading the Qur'an.

Othman left the question of his successor completely open. The rebels put pressure on Ali, the cousin of the Prophet, to become the next caliph. Despite the fact that Ali was ready to swear allegiance to other contenders he was persuaded to become the Fourth Caliph of Islam.

Ali

Ali ibn Abi Talib was elected Caliph in 656. He had married the Prophet's daughter, Fatimah, who died a few months after her father in 632 or early 633; the couple's children were the only direct descendants of the Prophet. The five years of Ali's Caliphate were marked by internal conflict. There had been those who from the death of the Prophet maintained Ali should have been his successor. Others, including Umar, were said to have been fearful of establishing a dynastic principal. Horror at the murder of Othman and then Ali's failure to punish the culprits also divided the Companions of the Prophet.

Two notable members of this group, with the support of the Prophet's widow Aishah, led an open revolt. It was defeated in the Battle of the Camel near Basra in Iraq (656), so called because the fiercest fighting took place around the camel ridden by Aishah. Aishah was captured and taken back to Medina where she renounced politics and continued to live in the precincts of the Prophet's Mosque. Ali then made his capital at Kufa; Medina was never again to be the center of government. The decision to engage in battle with fellow Companions alienated sections of the community.

Ali's accession was again contested, this time by Mu'awiya, the powerful Governor of Syria and a relative of Othman, who sought to maintain the interests of the Umayyad clan. Mu'awiya had governed Syria for 20 years and built up a large and loyal army. The rival claimants to the Caliphate met in a protracted battle at Siffin in Iraq (657). When Ali appeared on the point of victory he was forced by his army to agree to arbitration based on Qur'anic law. The armies returned to base, while two arbitrators, one selected by each side, met to deliberate the matter early in 658.

What divided the community were questions about the meaning of authority and legitimacy, the nature and meaning of leadership, how God's Will was to be understood as working within human society, especially its institutions of leadership. These matters of dispute raised other questions concerning the nature and actions of the community, whether it was fulfilling its moral and ethical duties, and how it would rely on God's Word, what it meant to be a Godly community. The questions were political, philosophical and theological.

The issues raised were by no means settled. The arbitrators decided both claimants to the Caliphate should stand down and a new election be held. This solution was no solution and only increased the bitterness between the factions. Some who had supported Ali then seceded and became known as the *Kharijites* (secessionists). They considered that Ali had diminished the Caliphate by agreeing to arbitration. The Kharijites went on to develop a radical political and theological position. The Muslim community had the right to depose or even assassinate a caliph deemed guilty of a grave sin, political or other, they argued. Furthermore, they suggested such grave sin called into question the status of the sinner as a true Muslim who therefore could be regarded as an infidel (*kufr*) and deserving of death. The Muslim community, they asserted, had the right to select whomever it wished as leader, whoever dealt with the people according to the precepts of justice and injustice was the rightful Imam, or Caliph. Ali moved swiftly to suppress the group in a bloody massacre at Nahrawan in 658. The Muslim world or Empire was effectively split. Mu'awiya continued to govern independently in Syria where, in 660, he proclaimed himself Caliph in defiance of Ali.

The Kharijites were not eradicated; indeed their ideas recur in many guises throughout Muslim history. In 661 they planned to assassinate the three most prominent leaders of the community: Amr, Governor of Egypt, Mu'awiya, Governor of Syria, and Ali. They succeeded only in the case of Ali, who in early 661 was murdered as he entered the mosque at Kufa for morning prayers. He was buried in a spot some miles from Kufa, where the town of Najaf later developed as a major pilgrimage center for those who adhered to his party, the Shi'at Ali, more commonly known as the Shi'a.

The death of Ali was an abrupt rupture in Muslim history. The ferment of this period stimulated a variety of trends of thought as well as the growth of factions that continued to divide the Muslim community, and do so today. There had been four Rightly Guided Caliphs; each had acceded by a different means. They had established many precedents that all Muslims accept as authoritative, but not on the question of leadership itself. And this question was leading the Muslim community towards the tragedy of Kerbala – one of the seminal events of the formative phase of Islamic history.

Kerbala

The Muslim community was now divided into three groups. The majority wanted political leaders to be elected or selected according the principles established by Abu Bakr and Umar. A minority favored hereditary rule by the Prophet's family. And an even smaller, secular minded minority, with political ambition and military might, sought simply to usurp authority. The politically ambitious won.

On his father's death, Ali's son Hasan was declared the legitimate Caliph. He was persuaded by Mu'awiya, who had already declared himself Caliph, not to plunge the community into further conflict. Hasan abdicated and retired from politics, living in Medina where he died in 669, allegedly poisoned. As the sole ruler, Mu'awiya then moved to re-establish the Empire and moved the capital to Damascus, his powerbase. Internal friction had been accompanied by continued hostilities with the Byzantine Empire. As civil war was suppressed, often ruthlessly, renewed attention was turned to external problems and expansion of the Empire resumed after a 10-year hiatus. Exploratory raids were made from Egypt across North Africa. The garrison town of Qairouan, in modern Tunisia, was founded in 670: later it developed into city and became a leading center of education. In the same year the first Muslim assault on the Byzantine capital, Constantinople (now Istanbul), was made. Successive attacks were made over the centuries, but the city did not finally fall into Muslim hands until the Ottoman conquest in 1453.

In 679 Mu'awiya nominated his son Yezid his heir apparent to succeed to the Caliphate. So it was the Umayyads in the person of Mu'awiya, the son of Abu Sufyan for so long leader of the opposition to Prophet Muhammad, who first put into practice the principle of dynastic succession. When Mu'awiya died the following year his son was acclaimed Caliph in Damascus. Many questioned Yezid's fitness to rule because of his dubious character, reopening all the varied political, spiritual and doctrinal questions about leadership. The questions were not confined solely to supporters of Ali, but the focus of alternative leadership fell on Hussain, the last surviving son of Ali, grandson of the Prophet.

Hussain took up arms against Yezid. At Kerbala, a short distance from Baghdad, Hussain and his 600 followers were besieged by an Umayyad army of 6,000. After fruitless negotiations lasting six days, during which his small force was trapped without access to water, Hussain finally rode out to meet the opposing army and was killed. Only two of his children survived the massacre that followed. The traumatic event of Kerbala established the Shi'a as the second major sect of Islam.

The Shi'a

After Kerbala the elaboration of Shi'a doctrine developed and diverged from that of the Sunnis. The term Sunni, derives from *Sunnah*, and is often translated as orthodox Muslims – these are the majority who supported the idea of an election or selection after the

murder of Ali. In contrast, the Shi'a believe in hereditary spiritual leadership known as *Imamate*. They hold
that Ali had a special spiritual function alongside the
Prophet which gave him an absolute right to succeed to
spiritual leadership, a right inherited by his sons. The
Imam is recipient of spiritual and political pre-emi-
nence by virtue of possessing special grace, miraculous
power and special knowledge. Shi'ism has developed
its own schools of thought, elaborate philosophy and
mystical tradition as well as schools of law.

There are numerous subdivisions within Shi'ism,
distinguished by the number of Imams each subdivi-
sion recognizes: the Fivers, known as *Zaydis*; the
Seveners, more familiar as the *Isma'ilis* whose leader is
the Aga Khan. Twelve-Imam Shi'ism became the official religion of Iran when the Safavid dynasty came to
power in 1501. After 500 years Iranian Shi'ism has
built up the most organized and developed body of
theory and practice. Iranian Shi'ism permits a much
stronger tradition of authoritative interpretation by
religious scholars, known as *mujtahids*, from among
whom individuals who have attained a certain degree
of knowledge are recognized by the community as
ayatollahs. This has permitted both an ongoing
process of *ijtihad*, reasoned struggle to reach contemporary interpretations of Islamic principle, and
greater flexibility in Shi'a thinking. Each ayatollah has
his own followers. When ayatollahs differ in their
interpretations and teaching, these differences are
binding only on those who have chosen to follow
them.

Shi'ism has remained a minority branch of Muslim
civilization accounting for only about 10 per cent of
Muslims. It was viewed with hostility by Umayyad and
later Abbasid rulers (descendents of one of Prophet
Muhammad's uncles, Abbas) who saw it as a potential
threat. But it is accepted as within the framework of
Islam by Sunni Muslims because of the acceptance of
the same basic principles and precepts. The concept

of consensus, keeping the community united and avoiding *bida*, innovation – that is, divergence from the example and practice of the Prophet – is central to the Sunni outlook. For the Sunni an imam is the term applied to the person who leads the congregational prayer, and therefore the term for an official of each mosque. Occasionally, it is an honorific for an especially eminent scholar, as in the case of Imam Bukhari, the compiler of one of the major collections of *hadith*. The issue of hereditary leadership, whether in empires, nation states or spiritual matters, is a debatable topic and not an accepted principle among Sunni thinkers.

The details of Hussain's death at Kerbala are re-enacted every year in the *Ta'iziyyah*, the Shi'a martyrdom play. The day of Kerbala, the 10th day of the month of Muharram, is known as *Ashura*. It was originally instituted as a day of fasting by Prophet Muhammad. Among the Shi'a it is a day of mourning and commemoration when certain groups parade the streets mortifying themselves with self-inflicted wounds as an expression of guilt for having abandoned Imam Hussain in his hour of need. Kerbala is the principal site of Shi'a pilgrimage. Many Shi'a place their heads on a tablet of Kerbala clay when they pray.

Under the Umayyads, Islam moved into an expansionary phase.

4 Expansion and empires

The rapid rise of Islam throughout the world has perplexed historians. The common belief is that Islam expanded through conquest. But trade and Sufi movements played an equally important part in its spread.

THE UMAYYAD DYNASTY ruled from 661-750. Their rule was despotic and unpopular right from the beginning. However, a great deal of the history of the Umayyads was written by their vanquishers, the Abbasids (749-1258) which may well contribute to the bad press they receive. The rebellion against Umayyad rule began in Khurasan in eastern Persia in 747, when Abu Muslim, a lieutenant of the Abbasid clan unfurled his banner reading: 'Leave is given to those who fight because they were wronged' (The Quran: 22:39).

The Abbasids moved the capital from Damascus to the newly created city of Baghdad in 762. Science, philosophy, medicine and education flourished under the Abbasids, who synthesized Persian learning with Greek heritage to fashion a unique Muslim culture. The Baghdad of Harun al-Rashid, who ruled from 786-809, is not only the setting of *The Thousand and One Nights*, the vision of a rich and splendid epoch, it is considered to be the Golden Age of Islam scholarship. The Abbasids were overthrown by the Mongol invasion of 1258: the Mongols ransacked Baghdad and burnt down its famous libraries. While the Abbasids claimed the Caliphate, the Muslim world was in fact no longer one empire. A network of regional empires had emerged, some making rival claims to the Caliphate while others offered it only nominal allegiance.

By the middle of the 8th century, Umayyad rule had already extended Muslim presence across the whole of North Africa. Territorial expansion of Muslim rule is one part of the creation of what is today called the Muslim world. The spread of Islam as the religion of the majority of inhabitants is a separate process that was seldom as complete; minority religions and communities continued to exist. 'Empire' is a loaded term in modern parlance. In history it is a varied, often negative but always complex development. However, the rise of a new system of political and territorial control often exploits pre-existing divisions and dissension.

What has been true of modern colonial empires is equally represented in the rise of Muslim Empires. For example, Muslim rule was welcomed in the heartlands of the Middle East where the oppressive regimes of the Byzantines and Persians created a population willing and ready to accept and co-operate with Muslim control.

On the other hand, the expansion of Muslim rule in North Africa met initial resistance from the indigenous Berber population, though they eventually adopted Islam and then spearheaded further expansion of Muslim territory. By 665 Muslim forces were using the Byzantine naval base at Jaloula, by 700 a naval base was established in Tunisia where 100 Egyptian families expert in boat-building were resettled. In 711, the Berber Tariq ibn Ziyad, commanding a large Muslim fleet and an army of 10,000, landed in the Bay of Algeciras in southern Spain. This force defeated the Visigoth King Rodrigo and moved on to capture Seville, Cordoba and in 713 Toledo. By 720 they had conquered all of the Visigoth territories to the north and south of the Pyrenees, the land the Muslims called al-Andalus. Muslim incursions into Europe were not confined to Spain. They extended into southern France: Narbonne, Nimes, Carcassone through Provence and the Rhone Basin. An incursion into France through Aquitaine was halted near Poitiers by the Battle of Tours in 732. This battle is seen by European historians as the highwater mark of the Muslim advance, a seminal event in European history even though it did not end the Muslim presence elsewhere in Europe. Al-Andalus, Muslim Spain, however, never encompassed the whole of the Iberian Peninsula and over the centuries was gradually eroded before the last Muslim sultanate, Granada, fell to the Spanish in 1492.

The Abbasid rule did not extend as far as Spain, where an Umayyad dynasty in exile was established. Other dynasties were established in North Africa. An Ismaili Shi'a dynasty, the Fatamid, emerged in 909 and ruled Egypt and parts of Palestine and Syria till 1171. They were replaced by the Sunni Ayyubid dynasty founded by Salahuddin al-Ayyubi. Better known to Europe as Saladin, he extended his rule from Egypt to Palestine and Syria from which he ousted the European enclaves established by the (Christian) Crusades (see chapter 6).

Another dynasty emerged in North Africa known as the Almoravids. Their name is derived from the Arabic al-Murabitun, meaning those who stand together for the defense of religion; the name and the dynasty originated as a religious revival movement. The Almoravids established their rule over a territory extending from Spain to the bend of the Niger River in West Africa. Muslim centers of learning in Spain were thus linked by the connective tissue of trans-Saharan trade to the university city of Timbuktu, in present-day Mali.

Umayyad expansion consolidated its hold on Persia and continued into the Caucasus, eastern Anatolia and Central Asia. From the province of Khurasan in eastern Persia they moved eastward along the trade routes to China establishing themselves, by 715, in Bukhara, Samarkand and Khwarizm, the modern Khiva in Uzbekistan. These cities of Central Asia were not only important centers of trade but also centers of learning that produced noted Muslim scholars. Imam Bukhari derives his name from the city of his birth,

Bukhara. The Turkic peoples of the steppes of Central Asia were renowned as soldiers and played a major part in the history of Muslim civilization. They also produced one of the most paradoxical institutions of Muslim civilization: the Mamluk dynasty. Literally the term Mamluk means 'one owned by another', a slave. They became a powerful fighting force employed throughout Muslim lands and went on to establish their own rule in Egypt in 1254. It was Mamluk forces that halted the advance of the Mongol hordes who sacked Baghdad. Mamluks continued to rule Egypt until 1517 when they were overthrown by the Ottomans, by which time they had become a landowning class.

The Ottomans emerged from Anatolia, taking their name from Osman, the founder of their dynasty, who was born in 1280. In 1301 an Ottoman force defeated the Byzantines at Nicea and began expanding into Byzantine territory in Eastern Europe. In 1369 they conquered Adrianople, the modern Edirne, on the European mainland. It became their capital and that meant the beleaguered city of Constantinople was surrounded. From their base in Europe the Ottomans advanced into Macedonia and Bulgaria. Their victory at the Battle of Kosovo in 1389 established their position in the Balkans. In 1453 Mehmet II, known as The Conqueror, finally took Constantinople – an event that sent shockwaves across Europe. Mehmet II went on to Bosnia, swept on through Greece and launched raids against Italy that had the Pope preparing to flee Rome – the threat subsided only with the Mehmet's death. Under Suleiman I, known as The Magnificent, Ottoman forces took Belgrade in 1521, overthrew Hungarian resistance at the Battle of Mohacs in 1526 and in 1529 arrived at the gates of Vienna. In this general advance they had captured Rhodes and established their sea-power throughout the Mediterranean. The era of Suleiman the Magnificent, 1521-1566, was the pinnacle of Ottoman victory in Europe. Under

Expansion and empires

Ottoman rule the Orthodox Church continued to operate while Islam gradually spread among the population of the Balkans.

Islam spread to Persia during the 7th century. The Abbasid Caliphs were impressed by the sophistication of Persian culture and adopted much of the protocol of the ancient Sassanid rulers. Persia was fought over and absorbed into the shifting pattern of empires established in the wake of the Mongol invasion. Stability was brought by the Safavid dynasty that ruled Persia from 1501-1732. The Safavid ruler Shah Abbas I made peace with the Ottomans, creating two great spheres of influence in the Muslim World. The Safavids became a major force extending the influence of Persian language and culture to territories to the east and into India.

In the west Ottoman supremacy continued to grow. It was the last dynasty to lay claim to the Caliphate. Sultan Selim I was ceded the title of Caliph after conquering Cairo, home of the last remnant of the Abbasid dynasty, in 1517. Their use of this title was viewed with considerable concern by European powers, especially by Britain which feared the emotive hold of the concept on the Muslim peoples it ruled, especially in the Indian subcontinent. British officials, backed by a battery of Orientalist scholars devoted great efforts to arguing for the illegitimacy of Ottoman claims to the Caliphate. The Ottoman Caliphate was ended by Turkish modernizer Kemal Attaturk in 1924.

The complex pattern of dynasties and the varying territories over which they ruled is only one part of the history of the Muslim world. Another way to approach the complex of geography and culture that is Muslim civilization is to follow the spread of Islam as a religion. The markets of the great cities of the Middle East were the hub of long distance trading routes extending over all the known world. Along these arteries of human contact, Islam spread

Major Muslim dynasties

The Umayyad	661-750
The Abbasids in Baghdad	749-258
The Abbasids in Cairo	1261-1517
The Spanish Umayyad	756-1031
Various Mamluk dynasties in Spain	1010-1205
Almoravids and other dynasties in Spanish city states	1090-1492
The Idrisids of Morocco	789-926
The Rustamids of Algeria	777-909
The Aghlabids of Algeria and Sicily	800-909
The Murabitun of North Africa and Spain	1056-1147
The Sharifs of Morocco	1511-??
The Ayyubids of Egypt, Syria and Yemen	1169-1462
The Mamluks of Egypt and Syria	1250-1517
The Safavids of Persia	867-1495
The Seljuqs of Iraq and Persia	1038-1194
The Ismaili Assassins of Alamut	1090-1256
The Seljuqs of Anatolia	1077-1307
The Safavids of Persia	1501-1732
The Ghaznavids of Afghanistan and India	977-1186
The Ghurids of Afghanistan and India	1000-1215
The Delhi Sultans	1206-1555
The Mughal Emperors	1526-1858
The Ottomans	1281-1924

through the agency of Muslim traders, peacefully and organically to many regions of the globe. Traders were often followed by Sufi mystics who established their own network of mystic circles. Where Islam was established new polities, states and regional dynasties were added to and became integrated with that complex whole referred to as the Muslim world.

China

As Umayyad power was moving eastward, the T'ang Dynasty in China was expanding its territory westward. The two forces met in the only direct confrontation between Muslim civilization and China, the Battle of Talas River, in today's Kyrgyzstan, in 751. The Muslim forces emerged victorious. The Battle coincided with the fall of the Umayyads and the establishment of the Abbasid dynasty, whose main priority then became securing their position in the Middle East. There was no military impetus to move eastward into China. The Battle of Talas however had a seminal impact on the development of Muslim civilization, one more important than dynasties and the control of territory. Among the Chinese captured in the battle were artisans who knew the technology of paper manufacture. This technology was avidly embraced by the Muslims. Samarkand became a noted center of paper-making and export. The industry was established in 793 in Baghdad, which became famous for its large publications industry.

Though Muslim forces made no further territorial expansion, Islam spread along the trade roads into China. The westernmost province of today's China, Xinxiang, is almost entirely Muslim. The land routes through Central Asia were not the only means by which the Muslim world and China remained in contact throughout their history. The sea routes of the Indian Ocean also brought Muslim traders to China. By the 9th century it is estimated there were 100,000 Arab merchants in the southern Chinese seaport of Canton (now Ghuangzhou) alone. Under the Sung Dynasty (960-1279) the office of Director of Shipping was always held by a Muslim. Apart from trade, Muslim scholars were also openly welcomed in China; there was an exchange of ideas in science and technology between the civilizations. Under the Ming Dynasty (1368-1644) Islam was gradually integrated into Chinese life to produce a distinctive culture outwardly Chinese but adhering to Islam. In the early part of the 15th century, when Ming China began to launch its own series of trade missions to the West visiting ports in Southeast Asia and India, the enterprise was under command of the Chinese Muslim Admiral, Cheng Ho.

India

The Umayyad expansion into Central Asia took Muslim forces to Afghanistan and in 712 they invaded Sindh, establishing themselves throughout the region to the west of the Indus River in what is today Pakistan. In 994 the Ghaznavids, a Turkic people whose name derives from the city of Ghazna which eventually became their capital, established a regional empire that extended from the eastern areas of today's Iran through Afghanistan and modern-day Pakistan. It was Mahmud of Ghazni who in 1000 launched Muslim expansion into northern India. In this initial phase Muslim forces were predominantly engaged in seasonal raiding into India, though in some localities they established more settled rule. Muslim political authority in North India was not consolidated until 1206 with the foundation of the Delhi Sultanate.

The history of Islam in the Indian subcontinent is complex. Trade across the Indian Ocean brought Muslims to the ports of the Malabar Coast on the west of India, where Islam had begun to spread by the end of the 700s. This was a region outside the orbit of Muslim-ruled territory in the northern Gangetic Plain. The Hindu-ruled South Indian kingdom of Vijayanagar which developed after 1340, for example, came to rely on Muslim soldiers as the backbone of its army. Sufi mystics found resonance with Hindu mysticism and Islam spread rapidly through mystical groups.

Cultural interaction also produced a cross fertilization of knowledge in science, technology, arts and crafts, literature and philosophy. This process was well underway before the rise of the Mughal Empire in 15th century. Muslims from many parts of the world traveled to and settled in India. The great 14th century Muslim traveler Ibn Battuta served as a judge in Delhi, as well as in the Maldive islands on journeys that took him to China. Muslim civilization was a creative conduit through which Indian ideas traveled outward and India received ideas and contacts with the rest of the world.

The Mughal Empire represents the last great fluorescence of Muslim culture in the Indian subcontinent. It was founded by Babur, 1483-1530, a descendant of Timur on his father's side and Jenghiz Khan on his mother's, who became ruler of Ferghana in Central Asia at the age of 11 and conquered Samarkand at the age of 14. He lost both possessions before setting off for Afghanistan where he seized Kabul and Qandahar before overthrowing the Sultanate of Delhi and establishing his rule in India. His descendants expanded Mughal rule over much of India. The last Mughal ruler, who by then had little real power, was deposed by the British in 1858. Today Muslims make up about 12 per cent of India's population. This places India high in the table of countries with the world's largest Muslim populations.

Southeast Asia

Islam spread to Southeast Asia almost exclusively through trade and scholarly contacts. The Malay world – the islands of Indonesia and peninsula Malaysia – was the place where the various branches of the extensive Indian Ocean trade met. Traders came in search not only of spices but also tin, precious metals and the other produce of this rich and varied region. The Indianized states of Majapahit and Sri Vijaya on Java were centers of Hindu and Buddhist learning long before the coming of Islam. The regular monsoon winds that brought traders to this region meant they had to remain for a period of months before a change in wind direction enabled them to make their return journey. It is through this pattern of regular, often extended interaction that Muslim traders and travelers introduced Islam to the Malays. By 1000, Muslim trading ports begin to emerge and by 1200 a Malay Muslim state was in existence in Aceh on the northern tip of the island of Sumatra. A succession of Muslim Malay states rose to prominence in succeeding centuries.

Africa

In the lifetime of Prophet Muhammad, as we saw, there was abundant contact between Arabia and the Horn of Africa. The Yemen had from earliest times been connected to Somalia, just as the Nile had connected Egypt to the Sudan since ancient times. Both these ancient connections provided means for Islam to spread organically through East Africa. After 900 Islam began to spread down the eastern coast of the continent into the region referred to as al-Zanj. It led to the establishment of a series of black African states in the coastal regions of Kenya, Tanzania – the name derived from the fusion of Tanganyika with the Muslim island of Zanzibar – as far south as Sofala in modern Mozambique.

These coastal trading states were in contact with the interior of Africa, from which they acquired such products as gold, ivory and slaves and to which they traded the produce of the whole Indian Ocean trading world. The trade in slaves was a feature of the ancient world that became a common practice in Muslim territory. As an institution little good can be said of slavery. However, there are significant differences between slavery within the ancient and Muslim world, where slaves were persons with minimal rights, and the chattel slavery, where they were purely property, shipped across the Atlantic to service the plantations of the Caribbean and the Americas. In no part of the ancient or Muslim world is a perpetual underclass of slaves or the descendants of former slaves found. The continued existence of slavery in certain Muslim countries in Africa, such as Mauritania, is less an anomaly than a disgrace.

The trans-Saharan trade routes linking the Mediterranean coast of North Africa with the riverine goldfields of West Africa below the great bend of the Niger river had also been in existence from ancient times. This was another artery along which Islam spread by organic means once the Berber and Tuareg traders who used these routes had embraced Islam. Trans-Saharan trade dealt not only in gold but also salt, hides and numerous other products. A series of black African states had been in existence since about the 5th century across the West African Sudan, the grassland region between the Sahara and the coastal equatorial forest region that derives its name from the Arabic *bilad al sudan* 'the land of the blacks'. The Dya'ogo dynasty of the Kingdom of Tekur in Senegal embraced Islam in 850. The gradual spread of the faith across this region became integrated into the life of the Empire of Ghana that existed on either side of the Niger river (not to be confused with today's Ghana). Muslims were widely employed in its administration.

Across the West African Sudan successive empires arose by fusing together and exerting central authority over differing stretches of territory composed of a network of cities and smaller regional polities. After the overthrow of Ghana, the Mali Empire founded in 1235, began its rise to prominence. At its height its rule extended along the Niger from the coast of Senegal to beyond the curve of the river where the major trading cities of Timbuktu and Goa were located, and on into the Saharan salt-producing areas. Its most glorious ruler, Mansa Musa, made the pilgrimage to Mecca in 1334. The Mali Empire began to dissolve under the rising influence of one of its vassals, Songhay which rose to prominence in the 1400s.

The great trading city of Timbuktu was founded around 1000. It was incorporated into successive regional empires but it was principally a city governed by its scholars. The city's most important institution was the Sankore mosque, which like so many great mosques across the Muslim world was also a university. Leo Africanus, the Muslim Moorish writer who was kidnapped by pirates and adopted by Pope Leo X had visited Timbuktu 1510-1513. The book he wrote while incarcerated in the Vatican after his abduction became Europe's principal source of information about the interior of Africa until the mid-19th century. Leo Africanus wrote of Timbuktu: 'Here there are many scholars, judges, priests and other learned men that are well maintained at the king's cost. Various manuscripts and written books are brought here out of Barbarie and sold for more money than any other merchandise.' Learning laid the basis for the civilizing influence of Islam, as described in the next chapter.

5 Civilization and learning

Islam produced a civilization with achievements in thought and learning, scientific development and philosophical sophistication that has few equals. Its enduring strengths were its civil society, institutions, and a way of living that defined the identity of Muslim people.

THROUGHOUT MUSLIM LANDS, dynasties produced noted rulers who, on occasion, were admirable, respected, learned and wise. Equally, they produced many a despot and tyrant who were ruthless and gave ample reason for all the political, spiritual and doctrinal questions about leadership to remain clearly in the minds of those they ruled.

However, from the period of the Rightly Guided Caliphs, scholars and thinkers were able to provide a framework of law and institutions within which civil society could operate and Muslim civilization could evolve. Study of the Qur'an and *Sunnah* for precept and precedent was the basis of the development of government, administration and the system of law. It also provided the model of domestic and family life, economic organization, and the modes of interpersonal behavior that shaped communities and even influenced the physical environment and ecological patterns in which they lived. The thought of Abu Hanifa, one of the founders of the Schools of Thought, provides a useful insight into the way of thinking that established the foundations of Muslim civilization. Abu Hanifa issued a statement of principles known as *Fiqh al-Akbar*:

> We do not consider anyone to be an infidel on
>   account of sin; nor do we deny his faith.
> We enjoin what is just and prohibit what is evil.
> What reaches you could not possibly have missed
>   you; and what misses you could not possibly have
> reached you.

We disavow none of the Companions of the
Messenger of God; nor do we adhere to any
of them exclusively.
We leave the question of Uthman and Ali to God,
who knows the secret of hidden things.
Insight in matters of religion is better than insight
in matters of knowledge and law.
Difference of opinion in the Community is a token
of Divine mercy.

After the bitter factionalism surrounding the end of
the era of the Rightly Guided Caliphs this endorse-
ment of legitimate differences of opinion set an
important marker. This, and similar declarations, also
clearly established the proposition that there were
moral and ethical limits within which thought, specu-
lation and belief operated. Abu Hanifa declined to
serve as an Umayyad judge. This too was a precedent
for many religious scholars who kept themselves at
arm's length from authority. By maintaining their
independence scholars became a repository of critical
reflection on the leadership of Muslim society, custo-
dians of the ideals of Islamic justice in the face of
tyranny and despotism.

Classical Muslim scholars were obsessed with the
concept of knowledge, which they defined and redefined literally thousands of times, producing elaborate
classifications. They saw knowledge and education as
the bedrock of Muslim civilization. Education became
institutionalized in the *madrassa*. Literally meaning
'place of study' the actual *madrassa* was more a resid-
ence for students, the instruction normally taking
place in the mosques to which the *madrassas* were
attached. Wherever Islam spread mosques were built
and building *madrassas* was the function of rulers who
provided a pension for the students, this being a recognized use of *zakat* funds. These schools were also
sponsored by merchant and craft guilds and set up as
private endowments by individuals.

Civilization and learning

The specific function of the *madrassa* was higher education. Students were expected already to have mastered the fundamentals of the Qur'an and *Sunnah* and committed the whole of the Qur'an to memory. In its fully developed form, established by the 10th century, the course of study included logic, rhetoric and law; traditional systems of mathematics; grammar, literature and history; the calculation of prayer times; and Qur'anic exegesis and recitation. In some institutions medicine and agronomy were also taught. The *madrassa* student would receive a certificate, an *ijaza*, which served as a record of their course of study and qualified them to teach the specified works they had learned. In parallel with the development of the *madrassa*, institutions known as *jamia* or universities also emerged, offering courses organized in different *kuliya* or faculties. The teachers in the universities were known as professors – those who professed original knowledge – and sat on 'chairs', the students sitting on the ground below them in circles. The oldest university in the world still in operation is the Al-Azhar University in Cairo, Egypt, founded in 970.

The system of education that spread throughout the Muslim world provided scholars with a recognized intellectual passport. The personal history of innumerable Muslim scholars includes moving from the domain of one ruler to another and finding employment as a *qadi*, or judge. The 14th-century Tunisian Ibn Khaldun, often called the founder of sociology and famed for his studies in history, lived in turbulent times that forced him to move between Tunisia, Morocco and Spain. When he decided to perform the hajj he stopped en route in Egypt and served for a time as Grand *Qadi* of Cairo. During his employment he was dismissed and reinstated five times, not an unusual fate: the holder of the post regularly came into conflict with the wishes of the ruler. The hajj, the pilgrimage to Mecca, was a common reason for travel, and provided a meeting place for scholars from all parts of the Muslim world.

Early intellectual and scientific developments were stimulated specifically by the practice of Islam. For example, the question of how to calculate shares in inheritance, as required by the Qur'an, was an ethical ideal that had to be made into an operative system and led to the development of algebra. How to establish the precise date of the beginning of the fasting month of Ramadan by calculating the phases of the Moon determining the Muslim lunar calendar was another necessary inquiry. Another was calculating the direction of Mecca, called the *Qiblah*, to which Muslims turn during prayers, from any place on earth. Each of these problems led to innovations in mathematics, astronomy and trigonometry that laid the foundations of the intellectual achievements of Muslim civilization. 'Algebra' is an Arabic word, and the foundations of algebra were laid by al-Khawarizmi in the 9th century; his name is the derivation of 'algorithm'. He also wrote the first manual on the Indian system of reckoning, around AD 875. The concept of zero was first developed in India and then integrated into the mathematics of the Muslim world. Building on the work of al-Khawarizmi, the first book including an explanation of decimal fractions was written by Abu'l Hasan al-Uqlidisi in 952-3. The problems of the *Qibla* and sighting of the moon led the famous 10th-century astronomer al-Battani to develop the cosine formula and to the development of the planetary model of Nasir al-Din al-Tusi in the 13th century. Al-Tusi developed a special mathematical formula known as the *Tusi* couple which later enabled Renaissance scientist Copernicus to place the sun at the center of the solar system. Copernicus also relied on the work of 14th-century astronomer Ibn al-Shatir who made major advances in the calculations of orbits of planetary bodies.

While Muslim intellectual tradition derived its impulses from the fundamentals of Islam, it was actually founded in the context of the learning of many civilizations. The centers of classical learning of the Hellenized Middle East, Persia, India and China were known to Muslims not only through territorial expansion but also by trading contacts. Peoples from each of these civilizations, with knowledge of their languages, culture and history became Muslims. As Muslims they acquired a common language, Arabic, that enabled knowledge from non-Muslim traditions to circulate across the length and breadth of the Muslim world. Furthermore, Muslim civilization remained heterodox, a patchwork of multicultural societies where Christian, Jewish, Hindu and Chinese peoples lived side by side with Muslims, maintaining their own traditions of scholarship in their own languages as well as adopting Arabic.

A great enterprise to translate the heritage of the classical civilizations began towards the end of the 7th century. The Umayyad prince Khalid ibn Yazid, who died in 704, is credited with sponsoring the translation of medical, mathematical and astronomical works into Arabic. The first translations of Greek philosophical works, including those of Aristotle, are attributed to Abdullah ibn al-Muqaffa, who died in 759, or possibly his son Muhammad. The translations were probably made from Persian editions of Aristotle's works. The Abbasid Caliph al-Ma'mun placed the translation of Greek and foreign works in philosophy, science and medicine on an official footing by founding the Bayt al-Hikmah, the House of Wisdom, in Baghdad in 830.

The Bayt al-Hikmah sent missions to Byzantium to collect Greek manuscripts. It also housed a library, a successor to the Khizamat al-Hikmah, the library of wisdom, founded by Harun al-Rashid, 786-809. Public libraries, free and open to all citizens, became a common feature of the great cities of the Muslim world. The Khazain al-Qusu in Cairo, for example, contained 1.6 million manuscripts in 40 purpose-built rooms.

At its zenith, Muslim civilization supported a truly monumental book publication and selling industry. One of the most famous booksellers was ibn al-Nadim who died in 995. In 987, he published the *Fihrist*, a catalogue, which sought to provide an annotated bibliography of all the books available in his shop, running to many thousands of entries (see box). Each entry noted the number of pages in the text so that purchasers could be sure they were not sold an abridged version. The *Fihrist* was more than a bibliography: it included a section on the alphabets of 14 different peoples with a preface on the distinctive scripts used by different languages. The topic headings of the entries give an overview of the literary wealth of Muslim civilization. They included the holy scriptures of Muslims, Jews and Christians; books on the religious doctrines of the Hindus, Buddhists and Chinese among other non-monotheistic traditions; grammar and philosophy; history, biography, genealogy and related studies; poetry; scholastic theology, *kalam*; law and traditions; philosophy of ancient sciences; legends, fables, magic and conjuring; alchemy; and sexual manuals.

The bookshops were often pleasant places where purchasers could examine books, order titles they desired that would be copied by the scribes working for the bookseller, as well as meeting places where purchasers could enjoy conversation and refreshments.

Education was a recognized application of the funds of the state treasury, the Bayt ul-Mal. Another important application was for health services. The study of medicine and the development of a health system was a further major development of Muslim civilization. Free hospitals were the basis of this system: the first was founded in Baghdad in 809, and soon no Muslim city was without one.

What distinguishes these institutions is that they were hospitals as we would understand the term today. They provided free medical care to anyone who needed it,

Al-Nadim on the catalogue of his book-shop

This is a catalogue of the books of all peoples, Arab and foreign, existing in the languages of the Arabs, as well as of their own scripts, dealing with various sciences, with accounts of those who composed them and the categories of their authors, together with their relationships and records of their times of birth, length of life, and times of death, and also the localities of their cities, their virtues and faults, from the beginning of the formation of each science to this our own time, which is the year 377 *hijrah* (987/88). ■

whatever their faith or origin. Patients were assigned to different wards according to the nature of their illness. They were teaching hospitals, places where students learnt clinical practice.

Medical education, as well as the training of pharmacists, was regulated and supervised by the state. The basic set of surgical instruments, that would be familiar to today's surgeons, was developed within this system. It is illustrated in the medical encyclopedia written by Aub al-Qasim al-Zahrawi (c 936-1013). The first treatise on smallpox and measles was written by Abu Bakr al-Razi (c 864-925), perhaps the greatest clinical doctor of Muslim civilization. Inoculation against smallpox became a common practice in Muslim lands. The Canon of Medicine written by Ibn Sina (980-1037) became a standard text for the next 800 years, not merely in the Muslim realm but throughout Europe.

While state funds were invested in education and health there was another major institution common throughout the Muslim world that supported these activities and many other charitable undertakings: *waqf*, which literally means a standing or stopping. A *waqf* is a trust, commonly land or houses, assigned in perpetuity to the state, the income generated from the property to be used for the public good. The *waqf* were administered by a separate government ministry, and the proceeds could fund mosques, schools, hospitals, orphanages and a host of other projects. Many research projects, as well as individual scientists and scholars, were supported by *waqfs*.

The state was also responsible for regulating the operation of markets, through the institution of *al-hisbah*, which ensured that weights and measures were properly maintained. Trade was the lifeblood of Muslim civilization as well as its connective tissue, aided by the introduction of a standardized currency. The prohibition of interest, *riba*, in the Qur'an, and its insistence on written contracts to ensure equity and justice made commerce and economic affairs a recognized department of Islamic law. The ethos of equitably sharing risk affected forms of contractual arrangements across the whole range of productive activity from sharecropping to establishing business enterprises. The operation of these principles throughout Muslim lands facilitated the development of economic activity and financial transactions over enormous distances. Cashing a check in a different country, far from being a modern innovation, is derived from the normal practice of the Muslim World, just as the word itself, check, is derived from Arabic.

The Bayt al-Hikmah founded in Baghdad was not a place but the model for an institution that was widely replicated. This development was not only important for its role in promoting translations, it also promoted an effective science policy, the development of experimental science as well as providing a forum where scientists met. Attached to the Bayt al-Hikmah were two astronomical observatories, one in Baghdad the other in Damascus. Soon a network of observatories spread throughout the Muslim lands. The most famous observatory was in Maragha where al-Tusi established an influential school of astronomers. The various Houses of Wisdom served as a meeting place for scholars, scientists, doctors, astronomers and

Some Muslim discoveries and inventions

Algebra
Algebraic variable symbols
Analytical geometry
Animal Rights charter
Astronomical observatories
Astronomical tables
Binomial theorem
Camera obscura
Carrying capacity of cities
Decimal notation
Experimental method
Glass making
'Golden Mean' in architecture
Gynecology
Hospital
Asylum for mentally ill
Laws of reflection and
  refraction
Logarithm
Mechanical clock
Number theory
Ophthalmology
Paint

Pendulum
Planetary orbits
Public lending library
Pulmonary circulation
Sociology
Solutions to higher-order
  equations
Specific gravity
Spherical geometry
Surgery
Surgical instruments
The guitar
The law of conservation of
  mass
The novel
The rotation of Earth on its
  axis
Treatments for meningitis,
  smallpox and numerous
  other diseases
Trigonometry
University

mathematicians. Each had its own library served by librarians and copyists. Lecturers were provided to teach all scientific subjects and their facilities were free and open to the public who were provided with ink, pen and paper.

Both chemistry and physics were established as experimental sciences by Muslim civilization. Chemistry – the word comes from the Arabic *al-Kimya* – was established by the 8th-century scientist, Jabir bin Hayyan. The works of Jabir (Geber in Latin) and his contemporaries, al-Razi and al-Kindi were full of technical knowledge to which modern industrial chemistry and chemical engineering owe a great deal. Physics was established by the 10th-century scientist Ibn al-Haytham whose work on optics is now considered to have made a major contribution. He correctly described rays of light traveling from an object towards the eye – the reverse of the standard opinion of ancient Greek scholars. He was also the first person to devise a *camera obscura* (a dark room or box into which light is passed through a double convex lens, forming an image of external objects on paper, glass and so on). In his *Book of the Balance of Wisdom*, al-Khazini (d 1121) wrote on mechanics, hydrostatics and physics. The book included a theory of gravity, identified as a central force directed towards the center of the Universe (ie the Earth) some centuries before scientist Isaac Newton (1642–1727) encountered his falling apple.

Observation and experiment were the basis of science, but the natural outcome of this very 'modern' approach was the practical application of learning and experiment to meeting the actual technological needs of society. The books of Muslim scientists show they made improvements in many aspects of agriculture, irrigation and the manufacture and refinement of numerous products and, through publication, stimulated further creative responses in technological development. Writing in the 9th century, the Banu Musa brothers produced their *Book of Ingenious*

Ibn al-Haytham on science

Truth is sought for its own sake. Finding the truth is difficult and the road to it is rough. For the truths are plunged in obscurity… It is natural for everyone to regard scientists favorably. God however has not preserved the scientist from error and has not safeguarded science from shortcomings and faults. If this had been the case, scientists would not have disagreed upon any point of science, and their opinions upon any question concerning the truth of things would not have diverged… A person studying science with a view to knowing the truth ought to turn himself into a hostile critic of everything that he studies… He should criticize it from every point of view and in all its aspects. And while thus engaged in criticism he should also be suspicious of himself. ■

From Ibn al-Haytham's *Critique of Ptolemy*, early 11th century.

Devices. Out of the hundred devices included in the book, seventy-five were of their own design. When al-Jazari, writing in the 12th century, published his influential *Compendium of the Theory and Practice of the Mechanical Arts* he made it clear he was not content merely to describe former designs. He praised the work of the Banu Musa brothers, but produced his own designs rather than merely following their ideas. Glass, ceramics, textiles and dyes, paper and ink manufacture and a diverse range of instrument-making as well as the development of water- and wind-power, oil-distillation and mining technology were among the subjects that benefited from the attentions of Muslim scientists.

Agriculture became a science in its own right, *ilm al-filaha,* and had an enormous impact on the life of the Muslim World. The interconnections of the Muslim sphere led to the diffusion of a whole range of new crops such as rice, sugar, cotton, hard wheat, eggplant/aubergine and watermelons from Spain to Transoxiana. Scientists studied soil conditions, climate and irrigation as well as the development of agricultural tools, crop storage and preservation, producing innovations that overturned the agricultural practice of the ancient world. The Muslim agricultural revolution introduced new crop rotation and growing seasons. The technology of seeking water and water utilization were vastly expanded as was the land available for cultivation. By the 11th century Spanish agronomists were carrying out research and experimentation in the royal botanical gardens in Toledo and Seville. Agricultural manuals were widely published containing detailed studies of appropriate manures for different soils and crops.

Science and technology as well as Islamic precepts also had a profound effect on the built environment in which Muslim peoples lived. Muslim civilization advanced by building new cities and the glories of Islamic architecture from Cordoba to Istanbul, Agra to Samarkand are a visible legacy. But the impact extended much beyond the investment in grand buildings and concerned ideas about town planning based on carrying capacity, zoning of industrial and productive activities to avoid pollution of water sources, and provision of social amenities and services to the urban population. Study was made of the use of light and environmental conditions to provide natural heating and cooling of buildings. *Harams*, inviolable areas outside towns and cities, near watercourses and other areas were established where development was prohibited. A second concept concerning areas where development and exploitation were prohibited, *hima*, was developed solely for the conservation of wildlife and forests.

The moral and ethical precepts of Islam were an active ingredient in the approach to all subjects, including science. Ibn Sina for example wrote of poisons but regarded experimentation with such substances as unethical. Ethics also lent a distinctive style to Muslim works. The normal form of a book would begin with a reprise of the opinions of the leading authorities on a subject before the critique and addition of the opinions of the writer. The exposition of ideas was cast in phraseology and terms of reference making explicit reference to Islam and giving prominence to intellectual humility, what was known and humanly possible to know was circumscribed by human ignorance.

The most characteristic figure of Muslim scholarship was the polymath, the sophisticated scholar whose interests and expertise ranged over a diversity of fields. Jabir bin Hayyan, for example, not only established chemistry, he also wrote on religion and philosophy, medicine and astronomy. The mathematician al-Khawarizmi was also an astronomer and geographer who corrected in detail Ptolemy's map of the world and made original contributions related to clocks, sundials and astrolabes. The 9th-century scholar al-Kindi is renowned as the father of Islamic philosophy yet he was also a mathematician, physicist, physician, and geographer who wrote a treatise on music. Al-Farabi, the 9th/10th century commentator on Plato and author of *The Perfect State*, was an encyclopedist who contributed to the fields of philosophy, logic, sociology, medicine and music. The 9th-century geographer al-Masudi (d 957) was also a physicist and historian. Omar Khayyam is noted as a poet; yet his major achievement was in mathematics where he was the first to solve equations with cubic roots.

Perhaps the greatest polymath of all was al-Biruni, who during the 10th and 11th centuries wrote 180 works of which 40 have survived. He was equally well-versed in mathematics, astronomical, physical and natural sciences, was an accomplished linguist, a distinguished geographer and historian, and a competent instrument maker who made a geared mechanical calendar. He could measure the specific gravity of certain metals correct to three decimal places and wrote a monumental study on India, its people, culture and history. His approach to learning bore the essential outlook of Muslim scholarship, being founded on careful observation and experiment, respecting the culture and customs of other people, and always emphasizing his humility.

The intellectual climate of Muslim culture produced an extensive literary culture of poetry and *belles lettres* as well as popular entertainment. Ibn Tufail (d 1185), a noted philosopher in his own right, as well as serving as Vizier at the Almohad court of Granada, wrote the first novel as we understand it today. *Hayy ibn Yakzan*, the story of a spontaneously generated individual who learns to recognize God through reason, was later translated into Latin and provided the inspiration for Daniel Defoe's *Robinson Crusoe*.

Where did it all go? The decline of Muslim civilization has perplexed both Muslims and non-Muslims alike. Conventional Western histories presume the

The 'Brethren of Purity' on Animal Rights

So it was not long before men had captured a number of animals and were keeping them for their own use and making them work for them. And they began killing some of them so they could cook and eat them. Occasionally some men would go out to hunt the wild animals who lived in the woods and forests, or would trap them so they could have their meat for food and their skin for clothing; sometimes they even hunted animals just for the pleasure and excitement of chasing after them and killing them.

The animals quickly realized how changed their lives had become since the arrival of men on their island. They talked to each other and compared the peaceful freedom in which they had been living with the harsh and cruel way man was now treating them.

From 'The Dispute between Animals and Man', one of the *Epistles of the Brethren of Purity*, published in the 10th century; translated as *The Island of Animals* by Denys Johnson-Davies, Quartet Books, London, 1994. ■

inevitability of decline and write it backwards into the history of the non-Western world just as the inevitable rise and supremacy of Western civilization is assumed and projected forward. But the decline of Muslim civilization was as complex as its rise. Certainly, Islam contributed to its decline by losing the spirit of inquiry, and internal decay. However, the hostility of the West to Islam as well as colonialism also played its part in the downfall of Muslim civilization, as we see in the next chapter.

6 Islam and the West

The history of hostility and open conflict between Islam and the Western world is long and complicated. It gave rise to Orientalism, the specific way of describing, representing and controlling Islam. But there is also an equally long but hidden history of cooperation and coexistence.

RIGHT FROM ITS inception, Islam presented the Christian world with a 'problem' of three distinct dimensions. What was the purpose of the new revelation to an Arabian Prophet over 600 years after the crucifixion and resurrection of God's own son? This theological dimension had no counterpart in Islam. Christianity presented no problem to Islam as this contained within itself recognition of Christianity. Right from the days of Umar, the second Caliph, Muslims kept churches open and provided all the necessary guarantees for the survival of Christianity and its institutions. The strong military presence of Muslims on the borders of Europe produced the political dimension of the issue. Finally, the scholarly achievements of the Muslim civilization, particularly after the Abbasids, presented the intellectual dimension.

Europe responded to the problem of Islam with the Crusades, a series of religious wars lasting almost 200 years, from the end of the 11th to the 13th centuries. Towards the end of the 11th century, the Seljuqs of Asia Minor, who had already taken Jerusalem in 1071, were threatening the Byzantine Empire. Emperor Alexus I dispatched an envoy to Pope Urban II seeking military assistance. The result was the sermon preached by Urban at the Church Council of Clermont in November 1095. We do not know what Urban actually said, but we do know that his words struck chords with his audience. 'It is reasonably plain that he proclaimed that by undertaking an armed pilgrimage to Jerusalem the participants would not only bring succor to their Christian brethren in the East but would also acquire spiritual merit and earn themselves a place in paradise. Notions about pilgrimage, holy war, the threat to Christendom and the numinous sanctity of Jerusalem were not new: what the Pope did was to tie them all together in such a fashion as to make them irresistible to the unsophisticated piety of the Western European knighthood'.[1] Thus, knights as well as peasants, monks as well as children, began their march towards Jerusalem.

The First Crusade lasted four years (1095-99). Initially, Crusades were led by French and German peasants who began by massacring European Jews en route to Jerusalem but were easily defeated by the Muslims. The second force, consisting of four large European armies led by Godfrey of Bouillon captured Jerusalem in 1099. Thousands of Muslims and Jews were slaughtered; a Latin Kingdom of Jerusalem was established. The success of the First Crusade also brought political and economic interests to the fore. The Crusades then combined the idea of religious wars with wars of conquest. The Second Crusade (1147-48) led by Louis VII of France and Conrad III of Germany was aimed at the capture of Damascus. It failed. But it galvanized the Muslims who under Salahuddin al-Ayyubi ('Saladin') recaptured Jerusalem in 1187. In contrast to the Crusaders, Salahuddin treated the Christian inhabitants of the city with respect and dignity. The Third Crusade (1189-92) was led by the Holy Roman Emperor Frederick I and Richard I, the Lionheart, of England: that too failed. But the Crusades continued right up to the Eighth Crusade in 1270 and even included a Children's Crusade (1212) in which most of the children died en route to Jerusalem while the survivors were sold into slavery.

The Crusades played an important part in creating a European image of Islam and Muslims that has persisted to this day. The purpose of carefully constructed stereotypes based almost exclusively on hatred and self-imposed ignorance of Islam was to propagate and maintain the crusading spirit. Incredible stories about the Prophet Muhammad became popular throughout Europe. He was a magician who destroyed the Church in Africa and the East. He attracted new converts to his religion by promising them religious promiscuity. He died during one of his fits among a herd of pigs. Muslims, on the whole, were bloodthirsty, amoral and licentious. A whole genre of biography, epic poems and passion plays, known as *chansons de geste* (verses or songs of 'heroic' deeds) evolved to portray Islam and Muslims as the darker side of Europe. *The Song of Roland*, a French epic poem popular throughout the Middle Ages and one of the oldest of the *chansons de geste*, describes Muslims as pagans who worship a trinity of gods. It popularized the term 'Mahound' which was used by scholars and storytellers alike to describe the Prophet Muhammad as 'devil incarnate'. *The Song of Roland* begins:

> The king our Emperor Carlemaine,
> Hath been for seven full years in Spain.
> From highland to sea hath he won the land;
> City was none might his arm withstand;
> Keep and castle alike went down
> Save Saragossa, the mountain town.
> The King Marsilius holds the place,
> Who loveth not God, nor seeks His grace:
> He prays to Apollin, and serves Mahound;
> But he saved him not from the fate he found.[2]

Underlying the poem is the unspoken assumption that the world of 'Saracens' is a mirror-image of Christendom, structured in exactly the same way but inverted in every moral sense. Thus a valorous Saracen would have been an ideal *chevalier* (knight) had he been a Christian. When the hero Roland dies he offers his soul freely to the archangels. But when the Saracen Marsilius dies his soul has to be wrestled out of him by 'lively devils'. Such imagery sealed the perception of Islam as an ungodly and violent creed in the European consciousness.

The Crusades were the early precursors of colonialism. In Spain, for example, frontier warfare waged by the Christian kingdoms against the Moorish sultanates aimed to clear the land of its non-Christian inhabitants. Newly conquered territory became available for settlement by influxes of Christian colonists who often brought with them a new system of land use. The previous inhabitants who did not remove from the newly acquired territory were expected to convert to Christianity, the only recognized means to become full citizens of the newly enlarged Spanish territory. This ideology was not only exported to the New World, where it became the model for European settler colonies in the Americas, but became the cornerstone of the emerging European empires.

Colonialism

The process of European colonialism began in the Muslim world with the movement known as the *Reconquista*, the rolling back of Muslim territorial control in Portugal and Spain. It begins as an ideological movement explicitly understood by Europe as a clash of civilizations. The *Reconquista* was an alternate form of Crusade, equally backed by Papal decree along with the European military excursions aimed at wresting the Holy Land from Muslim control.

Knights from all across Europe came to the frontier wars in Portugal and Spain. Portugal completed its *Reconquista* in 1249, when Faro in the Algarve was taken. Among those who participated in the Portuguese *Reconquista* was John of Gaunt of England (who had initially set out to join a crusade to the Holy Land) thus creating the long-standing link with Portugal that eventually provided England with possession of Mumbai (formerly Bombay) in India. Mumbai was part of the dowry the Portuguese princess Catherine Braganza brought to her marriage to Charles II of England.

The Portuguese appetite for expansion then became insatiable. During the 14th century, the kings of Portugal sought no less than five Papal bulls (decrees) of Crusade for plans to conquer Morocco and Granada. Extending the logic which began with Urban II, these bulls provided justification for the overarching ideology of European expansion. The Bull *Dum Diversas* of 1452 granted to King Alfonso of Portugal set out the terms used by all European monarchs who authorized speculative voyages of exploration. *Dum Diversas* was the warrant 'to invade, search out, capture, vanquish and subdue all Saracens and pagans... and other enemies of Christ' whose property could be taken and their persons 'reduced to perpetual slavery'. It was written by Pope Nicholas V who was at the same time concerned with trying to establish a rapprochement with Eastern Orthodox Christianity (Byzantium) so that together they could renew the eastern Crusade against the expansionary Ottoman Empire. The following year, 1453, Constantinople fell to the Ottomans. Nicholas failed to stir Europe to another eastern crusade. The immediate beneficiary of the crusading impulse of a fearful Europe was Spain in its campaign against the last remaining Muslim sultanate, Granada.

In 1492 Granada fell to the victorious forces of Ferdinand and Isabella, the Most Catholic Monarchs of Spain. Weeks later they gave royal warrant to the Italian explorer Columbus for his voyage across the Atlantic. The day after Columbus set sail from Spain was the date by which all Jews were expelled from Spain, their property and lands having been confiscated. In 1502 the same fate befell Spain's remaining Muslim population. The Bull *Inter Cetera* granted to Ferdinand and Isabella in 1493 by Pope Alexander VI continued the terms of *Dum Diversas* by expressing the Pope's desire that 'all barbarous nations be overthrown'. It was a precursor to the negotiations that a month later produced the Treaty of Tordesillas by which the Pope divided the rights to exploration and acquisition of all newfound territory around the globe between Spain and Portugal.

The pace and form of colonialism differed from colony to colony and among the different European nations. Contending for colonial possessions and dominance in the trade it generated was the extension of European rivalries onto a global stage. The history of colonialism is most often written and viewed through the gaze of these European preoccupations leaving out the ramifications and impact on the colonized. The eastward expansion of Europe into lands of the Muslim world overwrites and obscures a long and crucial period when there was no clear inevitability to the rise of Europe. Europe achieved its footholds in the Muslim world not because of superior technology and enterprise, as is commonly believed, but in large measure as a result of knowledge acquired from Muslim civilization. European powers retained their footholds because they were tolerated as small-scale new arrivals within the diversity of a complex and long-established trading world.

Portugal arrived in India and promptly declared the Indian Ocean a closed sea where all trade would be policed by its armed galleons, a singular new development in the Indian Ocean. It was an effective offensive threat since Portuguese vessels designed for Atlantic waters rode higher in the water than Asian ships, so their guns could bear down on native ships. Portugal moved quickly to establish a string of strategic defensive enclaves and decreed that all shipping had to proceed to these ports to be licensed to trade: unlicensed ships were liable to attack. Goa in India became the Portuguese headquarters but its next major objective was possession of Melaka on the west coast of the Malaysian peninsula, the principal port of the spice trade, which was conquered in 1511. Melaka was the center of a trade network and its conquest was considered essential for controlling the trade routes of the Muslim world.

Portugal and Spain were soon joined by England, the Dutch and France, as well as other smaller powers such as Denmark and Sweden, in contesting for trade and territorial footholds. The English and Dutch East India Companies – John Company and *Jan Compagnie* – were formally established in 1600 and 1602 respectively. In Asia, Portuguese and Spanish dominance was challenged and eventually supplanted by England which became the dominant colonial power from the Persian Gulf through the Indian subcontinent to Malaysia, as well as in parts of Africa. Holland took that role across the Indonesian archipelago, and France was dominant in North and West Africa, as well as Indo-China. Bestirred by its opening to Europe from the late 17th century, Russia also began a colonial expansion from the Caucasus through Central Asia.

The varied movements of European colonialism had a gradual and diverse impact on the Muslim world. The ideology of colonialism that grew out of the crusading ethos was rooted in the perception of Muslim civilization as barbaric, tyrannical, inimical to Western civilization and implacably hostile. Despite the fact that, objectively, Europe was at least no more sophisticated, learned or technologically endowed than the Muslim world, the notion of Muslim civilization as decadent, mired in superstition, a faded glory and with a particular problem in its treatment of women became a recurrent theme in European literature of the 16th and 17th centuries. Muslim power as a direct and real threat to Europe, in the shape of Ottoman expansion in the Balkans and up to the gates of Vienna was exercised as the foundations of European empires were established among Muslim

peoples in Africa and Asia. The productive and technological potential of Asia was not overtaken by
Europe until the Industrial Revolution when the pro-
tectionist policies of European domestic economies
were allied to purposeful colonial destruction of the
industrial capacity of Asia and its single-minded conversion into production of primary goods to service
European industry.

India, Indonesia, Malaysia, Central Asia, Mauritania
and Senegal were areas where early trading footholds
gradually developed into full-blown colonies. Algeria
and Tunisia were invaded and reduced to formal
colonies. Morocco, while never fully a formal colony
was the scene of successive interventions by various
European powers and American interests before
becoming a formal French 'protectorate'. The interi-
or of Africa had long suffered the destabilizing ramifications of European activities on its coasts – the slave
trade – but escaped full-scale colonial intervention
until after the 1880s Berlin Conference that settled
the 'Scramble for Africa'.

In this, the continent was divided into areas for colonization by specific European powers, the zones having been established by 'scientific' and missionary
expeditions undertaken by their nationals. The 'scientific' interest in the 'search' for the source of the
Nile became a precursor to British colonial possession
in East Africa, while French success in the 'search' for
Timbuktu opened the way for French possessions in
West Africa. From Senegal, where they had been
ensconced since 1638, the French expanded across
the predominantly Muslim savannah zone into Mali,
Burkina Faso, Niger and Chad. They also formalized
possession of colonies in the Horn of Africa, in
French Somaliland and Mogadishu.

Britain expanded from the Nigerian coast into the
Muslim north of what is modern Nigeria, and formalized its East African colonies including Sudan, Kenya
and Tanganyika, Zanzibar, and part of Somalia.

Britain also became the dominant power in Egypt, where it sought to protect its interests in the Suez Canal route to India. This also explains the increasing British presence during the 19th century in Yemen, Oman and the Persian Gulf States. By the end of the 19th century only Afghanistan, Safavid Persia and the Ottoman Empire were technically independent of colonial control. However, many regions nominally part of the Ottoman Empire and Persia were subject to considerable European influence and intervention in their internal affairs.

Colonialism from the beginning of the 15th century to the First World War introduced new divisions in the Muslim world, divisions of language, economic dislocation and new forms of economic development geared to primary resource extraction. It affected civil administration, social affairs, education and had a devastating effect on intellectual life. How colonialism worked to disrupt indigenous economy and society varied, but consistently worked to comparable ends.

In the economic sphere, for example, a pattern was established that still persists to this day. In Indonesia the Dutch used brutal means to establish a monopoly over spice production on plantations they owned and operated by slave labor. This included destruction of all the spice-bearing trees of Halemera island in the Maluku (Moluccas) island group to force the local population to seek employment on Dutch-owned and operated plantations. The introduction of plantations dedicated to cash crops became a general European pattern of enterprise across the colonized world involving cotton, coffee and eventually rubber.

When the late 19th-century rubber boom took off, Malay smallholders in peninsular Malaysia were the most efficient producers. They were systematically prevented from entering the market in competition with British-owned large-scale plantations worked by imported Tamil laborers. In Algeria, the French invasion led to the best agricultural land being assigned to French peasant colonists, the *pieds noirs*. In Egypt, the Mamluk authorities tried to revitalize their economy through investment in new cash crops, building up the local infrastructure such as irrigation and railways while asserting their power in seeking greater autonomy from the Ottoman Empire. These undertakings were enthusiastically funded by European banks, building up a serious debt burden. A considerable part of the debt resulted from the building of the Suez Canal, and the concessions that formed part of that project. Reliance on cotton production, the dominant cash crop, meant the economy was dependent on the fluctuating world market price tied, in particular, to the needs of the British textile industry.

The resulting debt crisis led to Britain buying the largest shareholding in the Suez Canal. It also led to European oversight of the Egyptian economy. While Egypt fulfilled all its obligations in repaying its rescheduled debt, foreign intervention in its economy and society steadily increased, leading to local opposition and unrest. The turmoil included British and French support for undermining the democratic institutions that had had been introduced as part Egypt's reform process, fuelling further unrest. In 1882 Britain invaded Egypt, defeated the rebel force and backed a series of puppet regimes that meant Egypt was officially independent while the real power was held by a British agent and consul-general backed by British troops.

Colonial powers also worked consciously to destroy the intellectual and educational structure of the Muslim world. Universities and colleges were systematically closed; Islamic medicine was outlawed; and Islamic science was declared to be nothing more than superstition and dogma. In Indonesia, the Dutch banned Muslims from pursuing higher education; a ban that lasted till the 1950s. In Algeria and Tunisia, the French introduced the death penalty for the practice of Islamic medicine, leading to the execution of many *hakims*, Muslim doctors. In India, the British established a new system of education to create 'go-betweens' for the rulers and the ruled. As Lord Macaulay wrote in the famous Minute of Indian Education in 1835: 'We must at present do our best to form a class who may be interpreters between us and the millions whom we govern; as class of persons, Indians in blood and colour, but English in taste, in opinion, in morals, and in intellect'. [3] And so it went on.

The increasing impact of colonial intervention meant administering the lives of the indigenous Muslim population by European legal codes and norms. Throughout the colonized Muslim world, Islamic law remained in operation only in limited spheres of personal and family law. This bifurcation had consequences for the education and operation of Muslim *ulema*, the religious scholars, and worked to reinforce the conservational paradigm that was making itself felt as European intervention began. Islam became an effective rallying point for many resistance movements that opposed colonial encroachment.

The need to defend Islam was most effective as a call to support publicly accepted received authority, unquestioned tradition. External pressure reinforced and empowered the ossification of tradition. The more Islam was marginalized to operate only in the sphere of personal and family law the less impetus there was to apply the pressing questions of contemporary life to the scrutiny of the Islamic worldview. The subtle redefinition of Muslim education to the study of religion in a narrow sense, that had initially been more apparent than real, gradually became very real and highly apparent as the division between a modern sector created under the dominance of European power and a traditional sector that was everywhere marginalized. Internal trends in Muslim society worked to increase the distinctions between

traditional and modern as they redefined and solidi-
fied what was meant and taught as traditional Islam.

Orientalism

Colonialism gave a new lease of life to the essential
features of the medieval representation of Islam and
Muslims. During the period known in Europe as the
Age of Discovery, representation of Islam acquired a
coherent structure and became an integral part of
European scholarship across a new range of disci-
plines such as anthropology and political science. The
tradition and scholarship by which Western civilization represents and perceives Islam and Muslims
came to be known as Orientalism.

The term was made popular by the noted
Palestinian academic Edward Said, but it existed long
before the publication of his book *Orientalism* in 1978.
Within the literary conventions of 18th and 19th century colonialism, Said found a consistent set of ideas,
a cultural imperialist code by which the West
described, investigated and presented its view of the
East as fact, a function of the nature of the Oriental
who is knowable through neutral, objective scholarship. Said described Orientalism as an overarching
style of thought, with a history going back to antiquity, based on the ontological and epistemological distinction between the 'Orient' and the 'Occident'. It
was a particular 'Western style for dominating,
restructuring, and having authority over the Orient'.
Orientalism was a 'corporate enterprise' that used a
'system of representation framed by a whole set of
forces that brought the Orient into Western learning,
Western consciousness, and later, Western Empires';
'a way of coming to terms with the Orient that is based
on the Orient's special place in European Western
experience'.[4]

Said's concept of Orientalism is not a description of
its origins: as we have seen, these go much further
back in history. What substantiates Said's concept is a

coherent history of the transmission of a repertoire of ideas that has been documented by many writers. One can begin with the polemics of John of Damascus (c748 AD), a Christian scholar who was a friend of the Umayyad Caliph Yezid, who declared Islam to be a pagan cult and described Prophet Muhammad as a corrupt and licentious man. Then move forward to the production of propaganda and popular literature created to stimulate, explain and justify the Crusades. And next, move forward to the vast body of literature produced during the colonial period by scholars, travelers, and writers – known collectively as the Orientalists – that systematically represents Muslims as militant, barbaric fanatics, corrupt, effete sensualists, decisively inferior to the West; and Muslim lands a haven for sexual adventurers. Included amongst the Orientalists were the most respectable and noted figures of the Western civilization covering almost every field of human endeavor.

The scholars who specialized in Islam, and hence played a major part in giving intellectual respectability to racist ideas about Muslims, included Englishman Edward Pocock, the first occupant of the Chair of Arabic in Oxford and Simon Oakley, the 18th-century historian and author of *History of Saracens*. There was also George Searle, one of the earliest English translators of the Qur'an. The dominant theme of their works was hatred and open abuse of Islam. The first Chair of Arabic at Cambridge was established in 1632 and was occupied by William Bedwell. As a biographer of Bedwell has noted, 'The gratuitous venom which Bedwell expends on Islam at every opportunity, even in his dictionary, is striking in its intensity. A manifest exhibition of his attitude can be seen in the title *Mohammedis Imposturae* in the first edition, and *Mahomet Unmasked* in the second, with the recurrent title, "a Discovery of the manifold forgeries, falsehood and horrible impieties of the blasphemous seducer Mohammad: with a demonstration of the insufficiencies of his law, contained in the cursed Alkoran"'.

But such venom was not limited to scholars of Islam. Many of the *philosophes*, the founders of the Enlightenment – including Voltaire, Montesquieu, Volney and Pascal – demonstrated the same trait. And, not to be outdone, philosophers such as Hegel, von Ranke, Ernest Renan and Oswald Spengler worked hard to show that Islam was totally devoid of thought and learning. Even Karl Marx had some disparaging and plainly racist things to say about Muslims. And adventurers like Richard Burton, the famous translator of *Arabian Nights*; Charles Doughty, author of *Travels in Arabia Deserta*, and E W Lane, who wrote *Modern Egypt* in 1834, added extra layers of exotica to the representation of Islam in the West. They described a treasure-house of magic and occult, astrology and alchemy, hemp and opium, snake-charmers, jugglers, public dancers, superstitions, homosexual dens, women ready to satisfy every sexual urge, supernatural beliefs and bizarre incidents that defied imagination. While a string of noted painters, from Jean-Auguste Dominique Ingres, Henri Regnault to Eugene Delacroix, developed a genre of Orientalist painting that placed barbaric Muslim men and sensuous, inviting and submissive Muslim women on the canvas. Colonial administrators like Lord Cromer of Egypt and T E Lawrence, aka 'Lawrence of Arabia' who in reality was a spy for the British, turned these images and representations into policies.

Orientalism was thus a wide-ranging enterprise concerned with almost every aspect of life. It served both as a justification of colonialism – why the Muslim rulers and population of that region were illegitimate and unfit occupants and possessors of the place – as well as a strategy to manage and control colonial subjects. It was not something that was based solely on ignorance; rather, as British scholar Norman Daniels has suggested, it was 'knowledgeable ignorance',

Orientalism on film

Lives of the Bengal Lancers (1935)
Northwest Frontier (1959)
Khartoum (1966)
Midnight Express (1978)
Jewel of the Nile (1985)
Iron Eagle (1985)
Delta Force (1986)
The Sheltering Sky (1990)
True Lies (1994)
Executive Decision (1996)
The Siege (1998)
Rules of Engagement (2000)

defining a thing as something it could not possibly be, when the means to know it differently were available. Orientalism acquired its authority by making Muslims incomprehensible yet predictable.

But Orientalism is not something that only existed in the past. It continues to this day; alive now as it ever was during the days of the crusaders and colonialists. Its basic codes and structures can be found in learned books as well the popular press. It finds its outlets in plasterboard movie villains as well as strategic political thinking. We can see Orientalism in action in films like *Executive Decision* and *Rules of Engagement* which present Muslims not just as terrorists but totally devoid of any kind of humanity. We can read Orientalism in the coverage by right-wing newspapers of such issues as 'refugee problems'; and in novels like Salman Rushdie's *The Satanic Verses* which caused such an uproar amongst Muslims when it was published in 1989. But most of all the concept inhibits, constrains and provides an edge of fear and discomfort in the relations between ordinary people, the non-Muslim and Muslim populations of Western nations. Racism and discrimination in towns and cities across Britain, Europe and North America exists not only in the attitudes and actions of an obnoxious extreme fringe, they can be implicit in the commonplace attitudes and information of well-meaning and well-intentioned nice, sensible people. The demonization of the Arab and Muslim community after the atrocities of 11 September 2001 in the US had all the hallmarks of Orientalist stereotypes.

Happily the relationship between Islam and the West is not only one of conflict, antagonism and distrust. There is also an equally distinguished history of collaboration.

Collaboration

The contacts between Muslims and Europeans during the Crusades were not all hostile. Many crusaders returned from the Muslim lands intellectually enriched and loaded with manuscripts. During the first renaissance in the 12th and 13th centuries, the time of philosophers St Thomas Aquinas and Roger Bacon, the transfer of knowledge, literature and culture was solely in one direction: from Islam to Europe. It was in this period that European students began to go to Muslim seats of learning to acquire higher education – just as Muslim students nowadays come to Europe and the US to pursue their higher studies. At the same time, Europe began a major initiative for translation of Arabic thought and learning into Latin and other European languages.

Right up to the end of the 15th century, translation from Arabic was the main intellectual task in Europe. Muslim thinkers including ibn Rushd, ibn Sina and al-Haytham, who had their names Latinized, became integral parts of the rise of knowledge and technological progress in European life. Thus, it was from Islam that Europe learned the very idea of reason and how to reason; Greek philosophy, experimental method, and much of its mathematics; and how to establish universities, set up public libraries and run hospitals. The crowning glory of Europe, liberal humanism, also comes from Islam. In short, Islam taught Europe the true meaning of civic culture and civilization.

Islam and the West

The most shining example of collaboration is Muslim Spain. By any definition, Muslim Spain was a genuinely multicultural society; and the rise of individuals to a position of power and prestige depended largely on their learning and professional skills. Not surprisingly, it was a magnet for thinkers, scholars and learned people of Europe who came to study in Cordoba, Granada and Seville in droves. Muslim Spain was not only home to some of the greatest names of Islamic civilization it was also the place where Jews enjoyed their finest intellectual flowering since the dispersal from Palestine.

One of the foremost Jewish philosophers, Moshe ben Maimon, or Maimonides as he is generally known, was born in Cordoba in 1135. He codified Jewish doctrine in his *Mishneh Torah*; and his *Guide to the Perplexed*, written in Arabic, occupies a place in Judaism similar to the works of Thomas Aquinas in Catholicism. Andalusian Muslims did not consider Maimonides a 'Jewish' scholar. He was an integral part of the intellectual scene of Muslim Spain and, as such, was seen as a natural part of the Muslim community. The Jewish scholar Bahya ibn Pakuda, who lived in the 11th century, was deeply influenced by Sufi thought: his *Guide to the Duties of the Heart*, also written in Arabic, was an outcome of this encounter. The work became famous throughout the Jewish Diaspora. His contemporary, Solomon ben Judah ibn Gabirol, poet and neo-Platonic philosopher, also drank deep from the Sufi fountains of thought. His famous hymn, *Keter Malkhut* (Royal Crown), which concludes with a confession of sin that has been adopted for the Jewish Yom Kippur (Day of Atonement) service, contains deep echoes of ibn Arabi. The term used by the Spanish to describe the 'living side by side' of Jews, Christians and Muslims is *convivencia*: an experiment in collaboration that lasted over 800 hundred years.

Much of this history of collaboration and enrichment has been deliberately suppressed by Europe.

Being a British Muslim

My Muslim identity was developed over a period of time. It is grounded in my formative years in Oldham which has always been my home (both physically and emotionally). I was born in Oldham and no doubt I will die there.

My 'rediscovery' of Muslim identity came through Europe, by studying Muslim Spain. It has allowed me to become a better citizen, shaped my Muslim consciousness and taught me good discipline, manners and etiquettes. In truth, it has made me a better human being. Leaving school with no recognized qualification, Islam gave me the thirst of knowing and learning. It allowed me to prove to my school teachers, who thought I was not capable of studying GCSE, wrong; and gave me the confidence and drive to complete my Master's and to start a PhD. More importantly, it taught me the value of aesthetics and to appreciate art and creativity. My commitment in community activism, concern for the environment and my social consciousness is deeply rooted in Islam.

I do not have a romantic view of Islam. In fact, I am very critical, the questioning of my faith has led me to become more confident of my faith. I have a strong objection to South Asian or Middle Eastern versions of Islam in Europe. Like the Hui Muslim in China, I would like to develop a British Islam, rooted in the Islamic history of Europe. This is the only way Muslims will survive in the West. The young people that I work with have no 'social' contact with South Asia. This is made more apparent in the ways in which the South Asian traditional Islam is being challenged on a regular basis by assertive young male and female Muslims, both in the mosques and also in the public sphere. Some are more assertive than others. I have thrown away my traditional longi for comfortable *halal* boxer shorts when I'm in bed. ∎

Shamim Miah, Oldham, UK

W Montgomery Watt, a noted Orientalist of the 20th century, suggested this was largely due to a 'feeling of inferiority' on the part of Europe. The suppression of the extent to which Islam shaped and influenced Europe as well as 'the distortion of the image of Islam among Europeans was necessary to compensate them for this sense of inferiority'.[5] It is high time this history was retold, recovered for the benefit of both the West and Muslim civilization.

Islam and the West

1 Richard Fletcher, *The Cross and the Crescent*, Allan Lane, 2003, p 78.
2 Translation by John O'Hagan; available on the Internet Medieval Sourcebook   http://www.fordham.edu/halsall/basis/roland-ohag.html
3 Michael Edwards, *Raj*, Pan Books, London, 1969, p 151. **4** E Said, *Orientalism*, Routledge and Kegan Paul, London, 1978, p 1, 3, 41-42.
5 W M Watt, *The Influence of Islam on Medieval Europe*, Edinburgh University Press, 1972, p 82.

7 Reform movements

The decline of Muslim civilization and the onslaught of European colonialism led to self-examination amongst Muslims, and the emergence of a host of revivalist and reformist movements.

COLONIALISM WAS RESISTED throughout the Muslim world. The 1857 'mutiny' in India, for example, was largely led by Muslims – the names of Tippu Sultan and Haider Ali, who led numerous campaigns against the British, are particularly associated with this history of resistance. In Indonesia, there were periodic rebellions against the Dutch. In northern Africa, the French were confronted with a strong resistance movement that culminated in the brutal Algerian war of independence (1954-62), portrayed in the famous 1965 French film *Battle of Algiers*. But along with resistance movements, colonialism also generated a host of reform movements concerned with the internal reform of Islam. These movements wrestled with the ideas of modernity and tradition and sought to revitalize Muslim society.

One of the earliest attempts to address the internal decay of Islam was led by Muhammad ibn Abd al-Wahhab (1703-1787). Apart from uniting the warring peoples of the Arabian Peninsula he preached a return to the basic purity of Islam. His writings argued against all forms of superstition and in particular devotional cults venerating saints which he regarded as placing intermediaries between the believer and God. He stressed strict observance of the religious duties of Islam. One might argue that ibn Wahhab was the Muslim equivalent of the spirit and temper of John Calvin in Europe's Reformation, and both became the guiding lights of states formed around their religious outlook.

Ibn Wahhab found a sympathetic follower in Emir Muhammad ibn Saud of the Nejd region of Arabia, centered near the present-day city of Riyadh in Saudi Arabia. The alliance of doctrine and political power was cemented by the marriage of ibn Wahhab to the daughter of ibn Saud and advanced by the intro-duction of firearms into desert warfare. Puritanical insistence on strict religious observance among their followers was matched by their willingness to regard opponents as heretics and apostates. This enabled them to declare jihad against fellow Muslims, which would otherwise have been impossible. The expan-sion of Wahhabi territory after the death of ibn Wahhab brought conflict with Ottoman authorities and Egypt in the early decades of the 19th century. Ibn Saud established the Kingdom of Saudi Arabia where *Wahhabism* is the dominant – indeed the sole – creed.

A contemporary of ibn Wahhab was Shah Wali Allah (1703-1763), the Sufi scholar active in India. Shah Wali Allah promoted a reformed and more assertive Islam. His writings drew upon all fields of Islamic study and sought to rethink the entire system of Islam in a spirit of objectivity. His emphasis on social justice combined with popular mysticism won him an enormous following. In West Africa, Usman dan Fodio (d 1817) began a reform movement dedi-cated to increasing knowledge of Islam, replacing superstition and tackling the corruption within Hausa society. The author of numerous works on Islam as well as poetry, Usman dan Fodio began a movement to bring social justice to ordinary people and was noted for his liberal attitude to the role of women in society and his dedication to improving female edu-cation.

His growing following was seen as a threat by the rulers of the Hausa states and led first to persecution of his followers and then open warfare. By 1809 Usman dan Fodio and his followers had established the Sokoto Caliphate exercising its authority over all the Hausa states after a war couched in the language of jihad. The ideas and example of Usman dan Fodio extended beyond the Hausa states and was part of a revival and reform movement all across the West African Sudan affecting the Bornu states, Chad, Mali and the Senegambia region where it became the backbone of resistance to the expansion of British and French colonialism. It is possible that Usman dan Fodio's writings and example extended even to slave populations in Jamaica and played a role in the major slave revolt on the island.

The Algerian Muhammad Ali as-Sanusi (1791-1859) founded a further reform movement. It was an admixture of ideas of Wahhabism with the esoteric practice and organization of Sufi orders, a curious combination. The *Sanusiyyah* movement was a politico-religious organization that became dominant in Libya where it spearheaded resistance to European encroachment. As-Sanusi's grandson became King Muhammad Idris of Libya. Another reform leader who expounded his message through the organization of Sufi orders was Muhammad Ahmad ibn Sayyid Abd Allah (1844-1885) better known as the *Mahdi* of Sudan. Muhammad Ahmad declared himself the Mahdi, the Divinely guided leader predicted by *hadith* who would come at the end of time. The *dervish* order he founded had strong links with that of Usman dan Fodio. For a time the Mahdi and his followers managed to roll back British control in the Sudan by defeating General Gordon before suffering defeat by the revenging force led by Lord Kitchener in 1898.

Opposing colonial expansion produced localized resistance influenced by particular circumstances in different parts of the Muslim world. But the call to reform also had a pan-Islamic dimension, an appeal to all Muslims everywhere. This global dimension was founded on a call to return to the spirit of early Islam and a reinterpretation of the Qur'an and Sunnah in light of modern times. The leading names among these reformers are Jamal al Din al-Afghani (1838-97) and Muhammad Abduh (1849-1905). Afghani has been called 'the wild man of genius'. Born in Afghanistan where he received his education in Islamic religious sciences, from the age of 18 he began his travels around the Muslim world becoming involved in a diverse variety of local movements of dissent. He urged Muslims to engage intellectually with the ideas that underpinned European power, the philosophy and learning that stood behind the political, technological and scientific might of Europe. Afghani joined forces with Abduh, the *mufti* or leader of Egypt, and together they established the *salafiyya* movement based on the idea of using the first Muslim generation, *al-salaf al-salih* (the venerable ancestors) as a model through which contemporary Muslims could re-examine their predicament. It became a systematic philosophy of Islamic reform, influencing generations of Arab Muslims.

The Muslim Brotherhood was another reform movement to come out of Egypt. It was founded in the 1920s by Hasan al-Banna, a schoolteacher, but its leading intellectual and theoretician was Syed Qutb. A literary critic, Qutb collaborated with Gamal Abdel Nasser, the socialist nationalist leader, in the revolution which deposed King Farouk and established Nasser as president of the new Egyptian Republic in 1952. But the two fell out when Nasser refused to introduce sharia law in Egypt. The Brotherhood tried to assassinate Nasser in 1954. Qutb was imprisoned and tortured; and emerged from prison radicalized. In his numerous books, and particularly his commentary on the Qur'an, *In the Shade of the Qur'an*, Qutb argued for a pure Islam uncontaminated with modern illusions. He also called for a jihad against Western and socialist interests as well as against corrupt Muslim rulers. The Brotherhood was outlawed and Syed Qutb was executed – forcing the followers of the Brotherhood to seek refuge in Saudi Arabia and the Sudan.

In India, the call for *ijtihad*, or systematic original thinking, to revitalize Islam made by Afghani and Abduh had tremendous impact on the poet and philosopher, Muhammad Iqbal. In his *Reconstruction of Religious Thought in Islam*, Iqbal argued for a total overhaul of Islamic thought. It was his vision of a separate state for the Muslims of India that eventually led to the creation of Pakistan. The ideas of the Muslim Brotherhood were echoed in India/Pakistan by *Jamaat-e-Islami*, founded in 1932 by Malauna Abu Ala Maududi, a journalist and reformer. *Jamaat-e-Islami* agitated for the sharia in Pakistan and advocated democratic rather than revolutionary reform.

Collectively, the *Jamaat-e-Islami*, the Muslim Brotherhood and the *salafiyya* movement exert tremendous influence throughout the Muslim world. Books by Maududi and Qutb are widely popular among diverse sections of Muslim societies.

8 Contemporary issues

Throughout the world, Muslim societies face a host of pressing issues. Many of these have an overtly political dimension, such as the struggle for a viable Palestinian state, civil war in the Sudan, and post-war reconstructions in Afghanistan and Iraq. There are also huge humanitarian challenges: most of the world's refugees are Muslims, victims of civil wars, political suppression and the 'war on terrorism'. But by far the greatest challenges facing Muslims are internal to Islam: the issues of democracy, women's rights, Islamic law and the rise and spread of fundamentalism. These have trapped Muslim societies in a cycle of despondency and violence.

WHEN MOST MUSLIM countries first obtained their independence in the 1950s, a great deal of hope was placed on economic development as a catalyst for democracy. But the 'development decades' that followed were based on the established patterns of European colonial dominance. Independence did not improve the economic plight of Muslim societies. Worse: the new rulers of Muslim states did not come either from the reform movements, which spearheaded the fight for independence, or from the traditional sector, the religious scholars, who conventionally commanded the respect and loyalty of the populace. The political leadership of the new Muslim states was in the hands of Westernized élites who acted as surrogates for the departing colonial powers. The modern, secular ruling élite marginalized the traditional sector from power and ruthlessly suppressed all forms of tradition. There was thus a constant conflict between the Westernized rulers and the hopes and aspiration of the vast majority of the citizens who were more traditionally inclined.

The jihad in Afghanistan against Soviet occupation gave a new lease of life to the more militant elements in

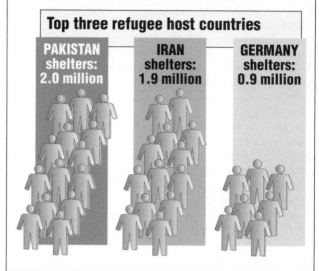

Refugees

The majority of the world's estimated 12 million refugees are Muslim. And most of them take refuge in other Muslim countries.

Top three refugee host countries

| PAKISTAN shelters: 2.0 million | IRAN shelters: 1.9 million | GERMANY shelters: 0.9 million |

United Nations High Commissioner for Refugees, *Refugees by numbers 2001*, www.unhcr.ch

the reform movements. The 1979 'Islamic revolution' in Iran provided traditional scholars with a success story and a taste for power. The militant *jihadis* who brought the Soviet empire to its knees, and who took up arms on behalf of their oppressed brothers in Chechnya, Palestine, Kashmir, Bosnia and other places, wanted to create an ideal Islamic state. The Taliban – literally student – regime in Afghanistan was an attempt to implement that vision. The fall of the Soviet Union brought a string of new nations into the fold of the Muslim world. So now there are some 57 Muslim countries; and an estimated 1.3 billion Muslims worldwide. But in almost every Muslim country, militant fundamentalists are making their presence felt and calling – indeed, in some cases openly fighting – for the establishment of an

'Islamic state'. They see 'the West' as an avowed enemy of Islam. Fundamentalist rage is directed as much against the West as against the modern and moderate elements within Muslim societies.

Fundamentalism

The 20th-century reform movements shared a common theme in stressing the need for a return to *ijtihad*, for sustained reasoned struggle to accommodate Islam with modernity. In contrast, the 21st-century fundamentalist movements are led by an entrenched class of religious scholars whose outlook is based on the fear of *bida*, or innovation. Fundamentalists do not want any change in how Islam was perceived and practiced in medieval times. But this does not mean Islamic fundamentalism is based on a classical religious narrative or Muslim tradition: in fact, it has no historical precedence. It is a concocted, modern dogma. There are two basic elements to this dogma. First, the fundamentalists confuse believing in the truth of Islam with possessing the Truth. Thus, their interpretation becomes the only true and valid interpretation; all others are *bida*, and people who follow such 'innovations' are not true Muslims.

By claiming their version of Islam as the absolute truth, they not only deny the manifest diversity and plurality of Islam, but also arrogate divine powers to themselves. Second, the idea of a modern nation-state is central to the vision of Islamic fundamentalism. Islam and state are one and same thing; one cannot reach its full potential without the other. Thus, all Muslim fundamentalists strive to establish an 'Islamic state', despite the fact Islam categorically rejects the idea of geographical boundaries and sees nationalism as anathema.

This fabricated dogma of Islam-as-State is a totalitarian enterprise. Virtually all Islamic states in contemporary times have been authoritarian and oppressive. Saudi Arabia, revolutionary Iran and the

Sudan provide good examples. Fundamentalist organizations themselves, as their names suggest, are minority movements that seek to exclude the majority from power: 'The Muslim Brotherhood', '*Hizbullah*' ('The Party of God'), *Gamaa-el-Islam* (the Egyptian 'Party of Islam'). The very nature of these insular movements, based as they are on the retrieval of an imagined 'pristine' beginning, leads them to engage with the world in terms of stark dichotomies: fundamentalism versus liberalism, tradition versus modernity, puritanism versus reform, Islam versus the West. Thus everything must be rejected; and everything must be based on the sharia, 'Islamic law'. It is 'Islamic law', fundamentalists argue, that makes an Islamic state Islamic.

Islamic law
Wherever the fundamentalists have acquired power, their first act has been to establish sharia, Islamic law. The sharia, as it is understood and practiced today, owes very little to the Qur'an; so it cannot really be taken, in Islamic terms, as Divine. The Qur'an, as we saw, has remarkably few rules and regulations: most of the Holy Book is devoted to elaborating the attributes of God and the virtues of reason. What goes under the rubric of sharia is mostly *fiqh*, classical jurisprudence, formulated in the Abbasid period when Muslim history was in its expansionist phase, and incorporates the logic of Muslim imperialism of the 8th and 9th centuries. Hence the black and white division of the world into 'the abode of Islam' and 'the abode of war'. This leads to the ruling on apostasy (religious rebellion) which, contrary to the unequivocal declaration of the Qur'an that 'there is no compulsion in religion', equates apostasy with treason against the state. Or the dictate that says non-Muslims should be humiliated and cannot give evidence in a Muslim court. What this means in reality is that when Muslim countries apply or impose sharia – the demand of

Muslims from Algeria to Pakistan to Nigeria – the contradictions inherent in the formulation and evolution of this jurisprudence come to the fore.

Moreover, the puritan fundamentalists are concerned largely with the crime and punishment part of sharia, or what is known as *hudud* laws. The word *hud* means limit; and *hudud* laws are the boundary or outer limit of the laws. A *hudud* punishment is the maximum and most extreme punishment that can be given for a particular crime. The sharia in the guise of the philosophy of Islamic jurisprudence, following the example of Prophet Muhammad, actually discourages the use of *hudud* punishments. Indeed, it insists such punishments can only given in a perfect and just society where economic opportunity for all and social equality are the established norms. So, the *hudud* punishments of cutting off the hands of a thief can only be given in a society where there is no need for anyone to steal and the state has provided all opportunity to make theft a superfluous activity of unmitigated malign intent.

However fundamentalists are only concerned with *hudud* punishments as demonstrable proof the state is enforcing the whole of Islam, not the parameters that define it; or with the notion of balance sharia demands. Their conception of purity means punishments have to be handed out exactly as they were formulated in the 8th century. Thus, the sharia is reduced to cutting off hands of thief, beheading culprits in public squares, and stoning adulterers to death. That is why, wherever Islamic law is imposed, Muslim societies acquire a medieval feel. We can see this in Saudi Arabia, the Afghanistan of the Taliban or Pakistan under General Zia. The fundamentalists' obsession with extreme punishments generates extreme societies.

Even though the sharia is touted as law, it can hardly be described as such. Law, by its very nature is dynamic and takes the moral evolution of humanity into full consideration. The argument within Muslim

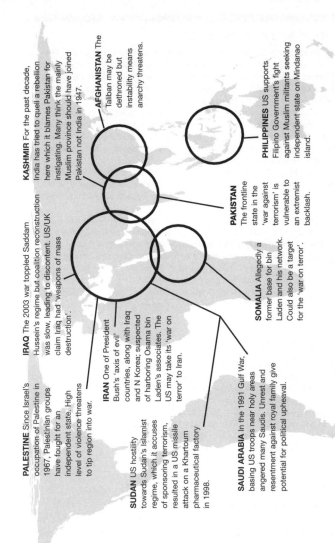

AFGHANISTAN The Taliban may be dethroned but instability means anarchy threatens.

KASHMIR For the past decade, India has tried to quell a rebellion here which it blames Pakistan for instigating. Many think the mainly Muslim province should have joined Pakistan not India in 1947.

PHILIPPINES US supports Filipino Government's fight against Muslim militants seeking independent state on Mindanao island.

PAKISTAN The frontline state in the 'war against terrorism' is vulnerable to an extremist backlash.

IRAQ The 2003 war toppled Saddam Hussein's regime but coalition reconstruction was slow, leading to discontent. US/UK claim Iraq had 'weapons of mass destruction'.

PALESTINE Since Israel's occupation of Palestine in 1967, Palestinian groups have fought for an independent state. High level of violence threatens to tip region into war.

IRAN One of President Bush's 'axis of evil' countries, along with Iraq and N Korea; suspected of harboring Osama bin Laden's associates. The US may take its 'war on terror' to Iran.

SUDAN US hostility towards Sudan's Islamist regime, which it accuses of sponsoring terrorism, resulted in a US missile attack on a Khartoum pharmaceutical factory in 1998.

SOMALIA Allegedly a former base for bin Laden and his network. Could also be a target for the 'war on terror'.

SAUDI ARABIA In the 1991 Gulf War, basing US troops near holy areas angered many Saudis. Unrest and resentment against royal family give potential for political upheaval.

Fundamentalist hot spots

Sharia law in Nigeria

In March 2002 Amina Lawal made headlines around the world. The 30-year-old divorcee was sentenced by the Sharia Court in Bakori, Katsina State in Northern Nigeria to be stoned to death for bearing a child out of wedlock. Charges against her partner were dropped when he retracted his admission of fathering the child.

The case is one of a number in which Sharia Courts have sought to impose *hudud* punishments such as stoning, amputation or mutilation. The word *hudud* means limit and is derived from the Qur'an though the punishments themselves are products of the development of Islamic law in history.

Since Nigeria's return to civilian rule in 1999, eleven states in the north of the country have instituted sharia or Islamic law. It is an intensely charged political as well as communal issue in Africa's most populous and ethnically complex country.

However, sentences handed down by lower sharia courts are subject to appeal. Also, they face political pressure and constitutional challenge by the Nigerian federal authorities who argue that Muslim Nigerians should not be subject to harsher punishment than other Nigerians. The case of Safiya Husseini, sentenced to death by stoning for adultery, was quashed on appeal. Amina Lawal's case is before the Sharia Court of Appeal of Katsina State and has been adjourned a number of times. The appeals process means such cases remain pending, defendants are bailed and no punishments are actually carried out.

The quality and training of judges, representation for defendants and procedures followed in lower sharia courts draw criticism among Muslims, who make up 50 per cent of Nigeria's population, as well as from federal and international observers.

It has long been a cause for concern among Muslims that while there is popular pressure for a return to sharia, ordinary people remain ignorant of their rights, obligations and opportunity to question the procedures within the system. While this remains the case the issue will continue to test the limits of the political and legal system of Nigeria. ∎

society is not merely for or against the sharia. It is a more complex and diverse cleavage over what is meant by the term sharia, and whose vision of it is to be institutionalized. As a conceptual term, sharia is intrinsic to Islam and therefore has a claim on the allegiance of all Muslims. For many Muslims it is a vague shorthand for their attachment to Islam as the source of their identity and their vision of social justice. This makes it an effective political slogan: to ask Muslims in general terms to oppose the sharia is akin to inviting them to vote for sin. But sharia as wielded by radical Islamic movements in many countries is an obscurantist (opposed to reform and enlightenment) body of rules and regulations, with little relevance to contemporary times.

When this reductive sharia acquires power it and its power-brokers lack the means and willingness to wrestle with contemporary dilemmas, they fall back on extracting the 'problem' of modernity from the equation by retreating to a supposedly pure, uncontaminated and truncated vision of civic existence. And its first victims tend to be women.

Women's rights

Those who formulated the legal rulings now popularly understood as sharia were largely men. While their intentions were good, and they clearly did not wish their opinions to be cast in stone, they were firmly rooted in their time. They had never known the Prophet and were directly influenced by cultural, intellectual and moral climates which were sometimes antithetical to the Islamic ethos. They thus moved away from the Qur'an's ethical codes for women's full spiritual, moral, social and intellectual autonomy and towards their culturally entrenched notions of women's subservience, objectivity, silence and seclusion.

Thus, the radical changes introduced by the Qur'an in 7th-century Arabian society were totally undone. The Qur'an provided women with explicit rights to inheritance, to property, the obligation to testify in a court of law, and the right to divorce. It made explicit prohibitions on the use of violence against female children and women as well as on duress in marriage and community affairs. Records of legal cases in the classical era of Muslim civilization provide evidence that these precepts were applied and upheld. Marriage in Islam is a civil contract. Historical evidence shows the great diversity of conditions women specified on entering marriage, up to and including the demand for sexual satisfaction, male failure to perform being a matter that could be pursued through the courts both as grounds for divorce and compensation. Property rights and rights to a share in inheritance made independently wealthy Muslim women, who were not obliged to share their wealth with their husbands.

In modern times an entire aid and investment organization has been established to attract funds from women in oil-rich states to support development projects in other parts of the Muslim world. Women were equally responsible for ensuring that all religious duties of the individual and society were fulfilled, in terms of punishment for social, criminal and moral infractions. They were also offered equal opportunities to attain the ultimate boon: paradise and proximity to Allah if they strove with all their means to 'establish what is good and forbid what is evil'. In contrast, the formulators of law could make women in law literally equivalent to material objects and possessions. When they considered women's agency, it was only in regard to service to men and family. Even in matters pertaining to women's exclusive biological make-up, the law focused on the convenience and inconveniences of men. The fundamentalists' sharia approach to women reduces the diversity of practice and interpretation in history to its most chauvinist, exclusivist and morally reprehensible tendencies.

Sharia-minded traditionalists, conservatives and fundamentalists treat women with contempt. For example, the testimony of women is considered – contrary to everything the Qur'an teaches – to be only worth half that of a man. Moreover, being a product of male perceptions, sharia law cannot distinguish between adultery, fornication and rape. As a result victims of rape and sexual abuse can find themselves charged with a crime and sentenced to be stoned to death – an aberrant law since the Qur'an does not sanction stoning to death for any crime whatsoever. Even though the Qur'an privileges women's testimony over men in cases of sexual offenses, in practice sharia courts choose to ignore them. In countries where sharia is the state law, women have worse than third-class status. In Saudi Arabia, for instance, they are not allowed to go out unless accompanied by a male. They may not drive, and have to wear a veil that by law must be black, despite the fact that black absorbs all the heat and is the least appropriate color to wear in a desert climate. (That's why men all wear white!).

In Pakistan and Nigeria, there have been a number of celebrated cases where women who were raped ended up charged with adultery – and, in some cases, sentenced to be stoned to death, although none of the sentences was actually carried out. Certain groups of fundamentalists, such as the Taliban who ruled Afghanistan and dominate the provinces of Northern Pakistan, even deny basic education to women. Statistics clearly show in general Muslim countries lag well behind comparable nations in female literacy and have worse than expected rates for the provision of health care to women and hence higher rates of perinatal and infant mortality.

The picture is bleakest for the weakest and most vulnerable women in Muslim societies, in general those who live in the poorest, most traditional and conservative enclaves. However, women's movements that express their aspirations for individual and social empowerment by appeal to Islam are to be found everywhere. There are women who regard Islam as emancipatory, and who use Islamic institutions and teaching as a resource to empower the poorest and most vulnerable of their sisters. Equally, there are Muslim women who endorse and support the conservative and obscurantist fundamentalist vision of the

Homosexuality

Most Muslims believe that the Qur'an outlaws homosexuality. In fact, the Qur'an is silent on the issue. The only reference it makes to homosexuality occurs when it relates the narrative of Sodom and Gomorrah where it describes the harsh punishment handed out to the people of Prophet Lot. Some Muslim scholars have suggested that this punishment was for 'doing everything excessively' rather than for homosexuality itself.

Classical Muslim jurists have tended to agree that sodomy is a sexual offense but differ in their punishments. According to Imam Abu Hanifa, homosexuality does not amount to adultery and therefore there is no punishment. But Imam Malik, who always takes an extreme view, insists that homosexuality is a capital crime and should be punished by stoning to death. This judgement is based solely on a couple of traditions of the Prophet; the authenticity of these traditions is doubted by some scholars. There is no evidence to suggest that Prophet Muhammad ever punished anyone for sodomy.

Homophobia and persecution of homosexuals is widespread in the Muslim world. Homosexuals have been executed in Saudi Arabia, Iran and Afghanistan, and capital punishment for homosexuality is on the statute books of some 10 Muslim states. In many countries, such as Malaysia and Indonesia, sodomy carries long prison sentences. In Turkey and Egypt homosexuality is not illegal. But Egypt was one of the five countries – which also included Pakistan, Libya, Saudi Arabia and Malaysia – which in April 2003 successfully derailed UN attempts to protect the rights of gays and lesbians. The move by the five countries was strongly supported by the Vatican.

Throughout the world, many Muslim groups, such as the scholars describing themselves as 'progressive Muslims' in the US and the Washington based network Al-Fatiha, are campaigning to reform Muslim attitudes to homosexuality. ∎

sharia and the radical political movements that espouse it. To see Muslim women only as helpless victims would be a mistake, one akin to the enormity of the most chauvinist male Muslim outlook. While the condition of Muslim women is not uniform across all Muslim nations and communities, or indeed between classes and sections of any one society the excessively patriarchical temper of Muslim societies is everywhere present as an impediment to democracy.

Democracy

There is nothing inherently inimical about Islam and democracy. Democracy, or indeed any specific concept, Western or non-Western, clashes with Islam only when it conceives itself as a doctrine of truth or violates one of the fundamental tenets of Islam. Only when democracy is wedded to atheistic humanism and lays claims to being the truth, or when secularism interprets itself as an epistemology or basic guiding philosophy, does it clash with the faith of Islam. As a mechanism for representative government, devoid of its ideological pretensions and trappings, democracy has no quarrel with Islam. Indeed, many concepts of the Islamic worldview, such as the notion of accountability and the injunction to consult (*shura*) the population, can be used to lay the foundations of democracy in Muslim societies and in modern complex societies can be argued to require democratic forms of organization and operation in order to function. But Muslim states, by and large, have chosen not to take this course.

Muslim thinkers have tended to reject democracy on the basis of two dubious arguments. First: the two are incompatible because Islam requires acceptance of unquestionable basic tenets and democracy insists on ceaseless debates and questions. As an example of the irreconcilable nature of the two, we have the frequently cited assertion that in Islam sovereignty belongs to God and in democracy sovereignty belongs to the people. This argument assumes Islam is a blind, unquestioning creed: an assumption contrary to the Qur'anic description of Islam. Moreover, it assumes politics is about relations between people and God, when the business of politics is one person's relation to another. But Western democracies are not perfect; many for example only belatedly came round to the idea that democracy and politics should include women. Democracies, like all other human cooperative endeavors, are also based on principles that are not open for questioning. On the other hand, religion is dependent on human consent, starting from its adoption and ending with its interpretation. Put succinctly, it is the people who determine religion, and not religion that makes the people. Democracy in a society where people are attached to their religious beliefs must reflect this fact.

The second argument is even more banal. It simply states that democracy is a Western construction and, as such, it has nothing to do with Islam and thus must be rejected.

There are deep divisions and animosities among and between various sections of society throughout the Muslim world. Most major political groups hate and fear each other so much they are happy to lose their own freedom to see their opponents defeated or shorn of their freedoms too. These divisions make it difficult to develop sustained democratic movements, since democracy cannot function without a broad consensus on certain basic issues. While an important aspect of democracy is uncertainty about the outcomes of the process, sufficient guarantees are needed that a change of government is not going to be a disaster for the losers. In Pakistan, for example, the leadership of the major losing party has ended up in prison or exile after every election.

The lack of consensus on basic issues has been further aggravated by open conflict between those seeking a more central role for religion in public life and those who oppose it. The growing support for fundamentalist groups, coupled with the capture of power by the Mullahs in Iran, Sudan and the now deposed Taliban in Afghanistan, has worsened the tensions and increased the worries of the dominant secular élite. Since the Algerian democratic experiment of 1988-1991 came within a whisker of putting fundamentalists in power through the ballot box, democracy has became a dirty word in Arab political ruling circles. The wave of democratization that swept the world after the fall of the Berlin Wall left the Muslim world untouched. There is not a single Arab state with even a modicum of democracy. Violations of human rights are common in despotic and authoritarian regimes, such as those in Saudi Arabia, Egypt and Iran. However, there are a few success stories. The democratic experiments in Indonesia, Bangladesh and Tunisia demonstrate that democracy can come to the Muslim world. In all these countries, a broad alliance of democratic forces, which does not exclude the fundamentalists or anyone else, has emerged to champion democratic reform.

9 Beyond the impasse

The spirit of Islam is seriously at odds with the contemporary practice of Islam. This much is obvious. Islam perceives itself as a liberating force; a dynamic social, cultural and intellectual worldview based on equality, justice and universal values. But in the hands of its most pious and puritan followers, it often turns out to be an oppressive and obscurantist enterprise, hell-bent on dragging society back to medieval times. Indeed, many observers can be forgiven for thinking Islam seems to have acquired a pathological strain.

MANY MUSLIMS BLAME the West for their current predicament. Indeed, the West has a great deal to answer for: colonialism, support of despotic regimes in the Muslim world, oppressive economic policies that have reduced many Muslim countries to dependency and abject poverty, and Orientalism, the representation of Islam and Muslims as the darker side of Europe and America. The list is as long as it is painful.

Blaming the West for their ills has almost become a part of Muslim faith. Orientalism, for example, has become a general scapegoat for everything. Among Muslims the existence of Orientalism has become the justification for every sense of grievance, a source of encouragement for nostalgic romanticism about the perfections of Muslim civilization in history and hence a recruiting agent for a wide variety of Islamic movements. It has generated a sense of exclusivity, of being apart and different, from the rest of humanity – a trend that has no precedent in either Islam as religion or Muslim history. Because Orientalism has been demonstrated to exist, then from the Muslim perspective by definition that which is offended against must be defended. That which is the subject of discrimination, prejudice, oppression and all manner of wrongs is thereby established as both innocent and good, no matter what its actual imperfections in practice.

However, Muslims cannot blame everything on the West. The internal problems of Islam are a product of their own failure to come to terms with modernity and interpret their faith in the light of contemporary demands. Whether it is the question of poverty or gender relations, democracy or globalization, the 21st century is full of challenges and new questions. These require new ways of knowing, doing and being for Muslims to understand – let alone to answer. Muslims are thus required to find fresh ways to keep their religion and tradition alive and relevant.

In particular, the tendency to fall back comfortably on age-old interpretations is now dangerously obsolete. This is not a new realization. Scholars and thinkers have been suggesting for well over a century that Muslims must make a serious attempt at *ijtihad*, at reasoned struggle and rethinking, to reform Islam. Ossified and frozen historic interpretations constantly drag Muslims back to medieval times; worse, to perceived and romanticized contexts that never existed in history. So the very ideas and concepts that are supposed to take Muslim societies towards humane values now actually take them in the opposite direction. From the subtle beauty of a perennial challenge to construct justice through mercy and compassion, we get ancient mechanistic formulae fixated on the extremes repeated by people convinced they have no duty to think for themselves because all questions have been answered for them by the classical jurists and religious scholars, far better men now long dead. And because everything carries the brand name of Islam, to question it, or argue against it, is tantamount to voting for sin.

This is why attempts to reform sharia law are seen as attacks on Islam itself. The guardians of the sharia, the religious scholars who were responsible for 'closing the gates of *ijtihad*' several centuries ago, have been particularly clever in declaring sharia to be total-ly Divine and equating religion with law. By collapsing law with religion, any effort to reform the law looks like an attempt to change the religion. Moreover, by appropriating all interpretative power in their own hands, they deny agency to ordinary believers who have nothing to do except blindly follow obscurantist *mullahs*, clerics, who dominate Muslim societies and circumscribe them with fanaticism and absurdly reductive logic. To change the sharia, and hence reform Islam, ordinary Muslims have to stand up to powerfully entrenched clerics and interpretive com-munities who see any reform as a direct threat to their monopoly on religious knowledge. By equating Islam with the State, obscurantist religious forces are also trying, and indeed have succeeded in many cases, to add political power to their religious authority.

Unless Islam is reformed, authoritarianism, oppres-sion of women and minorities, obscurantism and nos-talgia for medieval times will continue to reign supreme in the Muslim world. The way to a fresh, con-temporary appreciation of Islam requires Muslims, as individuals and communities, to reclaim agency. They have to insist on their right and duty, as believers and knowledgeable people, to interpret and reinterpret the basic sources of Islam. They need to question what now goes under the general rubric of sharia, to declare that much of *fiqh* is now dangerously obsolete, to stand up to the absurd notion of an Islam confined by a geographically bound state. The very survival of Islam as a viable, thriving worldview depends on these radical transformations.

The West has the task of learning to think different-ly about Islam and Muslims. The Muslim world must rethink Islam itself. It needs to learn how its values, its moral and ethical impulses are not a separate order but integral part of the common concerns of contem-porary human dilemmas. Muslims want sustainable development, human betterment, are concerned about saving the Earth, where science is going, how to attain a just, equitable and inclusive social and political order where they live and are worried about the downside of globalization. To these common concerns they bring a particular way of seeing problems. They have to realize Islam does not provide ready-made answers to these concerns. Only by working together, with mutual respect, can Islam and the West transcend their history of conflict and suspicion and shape a viable future for all humanity.

Glossary

Adl: justice, more particularly, distributive justice in all its various manifestations: social, economic, political, environmental as well as intellectual and spiritual.

Din: Islam's description of itself. In its primary sense *din* means a return to man's inherent nature. In general, *din* not only includes the idea of religion as commonly understood, but also the notions of culture, civilization, tradition and worldview.

Fiqh: Islamic jurisprudence.

Hadith: sayings or traditions of the Prophet Muhammad.

Halal: lawful, good and beneficial.

Haram: unlawful, and socially, morally and spiritually harmful.

Hijra: the migration of the Prophet Muhammad from Mecca to Medina in the 12th year of his mission in June 622 CE/AD. It marks the beginning of the Islamic calendar (the years AH) which is thus referred to as *hijra* calendar.

Ijma: literally, agreeing upon, consensus of the community in general, and the learned in particular.

Ijtihad: systematic original thinking; exerting oneself to the utmost degree to reach comprehension and form an opinion.

Ilm: knowledge in all forms, and distributive knowledge in particular; it incorporates the notion of wisdom and justice.

Islam: peace, submission to God, religion of God, the natural inclination of man.

Jihad: literally, striving. Any earnest striving in the way of God, involving personal, financial, intellectual or physical effort, for righteousness and against oppression or wrong doing.

Sharia: literally means the path to a watering hole; it is the ethical, moral and legal code of Islam. Conventionally translated as 'Islamic Law'.

Sirah: the life or biography of the Prophet Muhammad.

Sunnah: literally, path or example. Applies particularly to the example of the Prophet Muhammad and includes what he said, actually did and agreed to.

Ulama: religious scholars.

Ummah: the ensemble of Muslim individuals and communities forming an entity of common culture with common goals and aspirations, as well as certain self-consciousness, but not necessarily a coincident common polity.

Waqf: pious, charitable foundation.

Zakat: the compulsory purifying tax on wealth; one of the five pillars of Islam.

Timeline

569-649
Prophet Muhammad born in Mecca (569)
Death of the Prophet Muhammad (632)
Abu Bakr becomes First Caliph (632)
Omar becomes Second Caliph (634)
Expansion to Syria
Expansion to Iraq
Capture of Jerusalem (638)
Introduction of the Hijra calendar
Expansion to Persia
Conquest of Egypt
Othman becomes Third Caliph (644)
Expansion into the Maghreb
Creation of Arab Navy
Capture of Cyprus

650-700

Compilation of the Qur'an (650-652)
Defeat of the Byzantines
Ali becomes Fourth Caliph (656)
Proclamation of Mu'awiya as Caliph in defiance of Ali (660)
Assassination of Caliph Ali (661)
Umayyad dynasty established in Damascus
Mu'awiya I becomes Caliph (661)
Indian numerals appear in Syria
Introduction of Arabic coinage
Yezid becomes Caliph (679)
The battle of Kerbala and massacre of Hussain and his party (689)

700-750

Invasion of Spain (711)
Expansion of Muslims into Indus Valley
Crossing of Muslims into France (718)
Battle of Tours (732)
Umayyad dynasty ends (749)

751-800

Introduction of paper industry in the Arab world
The publication industry established as a sophisticated enterprise
The great compliers of *hadith* publish their works: al-Bukhari, Muslim, Abu
Dawood, al-Tirmidhi, ibn Maja and al-Nasai
Abbasid dynasty founded
Al-Saffar becomes Caliph
Spanish Umayyads established in Cordoba (756)
Beginning of the Mutazilite philosophy (757)
Foundation of Baghdad (762)
Ibn Ishaq publishes the famous biography of the Prophet Muhammad
Death of Imam Hanifa

Timeline

Charlemagne's Invasion of Spain; Death of Roland (778)
Blue mosque of Cordoba founded, Harun al-Rashid becomes Caliph (786)
Idrisids are established in Morocco (788)
Islamic Jurisprudence (*fiqh*) codified with six 'Schools of Thought' established

800-850

Ibn Hisham publishes his biography of the Prophet Muhammad
Philosopher al-Kindi established as the first Muslim philosopher
The first public hospital established in Baghdad (809)
Jabir ibn Hayan establishes chemistry as an experimental science
Imam Shafi dies (820)
Sicily conquered (827)
al-Khwarizmi publishes *Algebra*
Bayt al-Hikmah (House of Wisdom), public library, is founded in Baghdad (832)
The translations of the works of Greece, Babylonia, Syria, Persia, India and Egypt reaches its peak
The Mutazalite (rational) School of philosophy founded
The Thousand and One Nights makes an early appearance

851-900

Al-Jahiz, the 'goggle-eyed' publishes *The Book of Animals*
Philosopher al-Farabi publishes *The Perfect State*
Hunyan ibn Ishaq, the renowned translator, publishes translation of Greek philosophy and other works
Mosque of ibn Tulun built in Cairo (878)
The Ulama established as a major force against the State
Philospher al-Razi
Musa Brothers publish their book of mechanical devices
Al-Battani publishes *On the Sciences of Stars*
Al-Fargani publishes his *Elements of Astronomy*

901-950

Death of Thabit ibn Qurrah, mathematician, philosopher
Historian al-Tabari and poet al-Mutanabbi born (915)
Death of Al-Hallaj (922)
Al-Razi, publishes first book on smallpox and measles
Poet Firdawsi born (934)
Mathematician Abu al-Wafa born (940)

951-1000

Geographer al-Masudi dies
al-Haytham publishes *Optics* containing the basic formulae of reflection and refraction
Fatimid dynasty established in Egypt (966)
Al-Azhar mosque built in Cairo (970)
Al-Baruni publishes *India and Determination of the Co-ordinates of the Cities*
Poet al-Maarri born (973)

Ghaznavid dynasty established in Afghanistan and northern India (977)
Philosopher and physician ibn Sina publishes *Canons of Medicine*, the standard text for the next 800 years; and many philosophic works
The publication of *Fihirst al-Nadim*, the Catalogue of books contained in the bookshop of al-Nadim (987)
Al-Azhar University, the first in the world, established in Cairo (988)
The Ghurids succeed the Ghaznavids in Afghanistan and northern India
Humanist Al-Masudi lays the foundation of human geography

1001-1100

Statesman, educator Nizam al-Mulk born
Poet Omar Khayyam solves equations of three degrees
Theologian, thinker al-Ghazali publishes *The Revival of Religious Sciences* and *The Incoherence of the Philosophers*
Geographer al-Idrisi born
'The Brethren of Purity' and other Encyclopedists publish various encyclopedias, including periodical part-works
Muslims travel as far as Vietnam where they establish communities

1101-1200

Al-Idrisi of Sicily publishes the first detailed map of the world
Philosopher, psychologist ibn Bajja publishes *Ilm al-Nafs*, and establishes psychology as a separate discipline
Philosopher, novelist ibn Tufail publishes *The Life of Hayy*
Ibn Rushd publishes *The Incoherence of the Incoherence* and other philosophic works
Salahuddin ('Saladin') captures Jerusalem (1187) and unites the Muslim world with Egypt as its center
Al-Hariri publishes his linguistic masterpiece, *The Assemblies*
Yaqut al-Hamawi publishes his Geographical Dictionary
Poet Nizami born

1201-1300

Fakhr al-Din Razi publishes his great *Encyclopedia of Science*
Mystic poet Jalal-al-Din Rumi publishes *The Mathnavi*
Biographer Abu Khallikan establishes philosophy of history as a distinct discipline
Farid al-Din Attar publishes *The Conference of the Birds*
The Nasrids established in Granada (1230)
Mongols sack Baghdad (1258); the city's 36 public libraries are burnt
Abbasid Caliphate ends (1258)
The Ottoman Empire founded (1281)
The Rise of the Mamluks in Egypt
Ibn Nafis accurately describes the circulation of the blood
Nasir al-Din al-Tusi completes his work *Memoir of the Science of Astronomy* (1261) at the Maragha observatory setting forward a comprehensive structure of the universe; and develops the 'Tusi couple' enabling mathematical calculations to establish a heliocentric worldview
Islamic science and learning translated into European languages

Timeline

1301-1400

Ibn Khuldun establishes sociology and publishes *Introduction to History*
Ibn Battuta publishes his *Travels*
Islam established in Indonesia and Malayan Archipelago
Mali, Gao and Timbuktu become important Muslim centers
Poet Hafiz, master of the *ghazal*, publishes his poetry

1401-1500

Death of Jami, the last of the great Sufi poets
Islamic science and learning begins to be incorporated in Europe

1501-1600

Mughal dynasty established in India (1526)
Eclipse of Timbuktu as the Great City of Learning (1591)
Ottoman Architect Sinan builds the Blue Mosque complex in Istanbul

1601-1700

Taj Mahal completed in Agra, India (1654)
Islamic Humanism adopted in Europe

1701-1800

British colonization of India
Shah Waliullah establishes resistance against the British in India
Usman dan Fodio establishes the Sokoto Caliphate in Northern Nigeria
Muhammad bin Abdul Wahhab establishes the Wahhabi movement in Arabia, Syria and Iraq
Sayyid Muhammad bin Ali al-Sanusi establishes the Sanusiyyah movement in North Africa

1801-1900

'Indian Mutiny' (1857)
Jamal al-Din Al-Afghani, Muhammad Abduh and Rashid Rida establish the pan-Islamic movement
Sir Syed Ahmad Khan establishes the Muslim University of Aligrah, India (1875)

1901-2000

Kemal Ataturk ends Caliphate (1914)
Rise of Nationalism in the Muslim World
Poet and philosopher Muhammad Iqbal publishes *Complaint and Answer*
Pakistan created as the first 'Islamic state' (1947)
Organization of Islamic Conference (OIC) established (1969)
Emergence of OPEC (1972)
'Islamic revolution' in Iran (1979)

Bibliography

The Koran Interpreted by A J Arberry (Oxford University Press, 1964).

The Meaning of the Glorious Koran by M M Pickthall (various editions).

Introducing Islam by Ziauddin Sardar and Zafar Abbas Malik (Icon Books, 2002).

On Being a Muslim by Farid Esack (One World, 1999).

Revival and Reform in Islam by Fazlur Rahman (One World, 2000).

Women in the Qur'an by Amina Wadud (Oxford University Press, 1999).

'Believing Women' in Islam by Asma Barlas (University of Texas Press, 2002).

Orientalism by Ziauddin Sardar (Open University Press, 1999).

The Crusades Through Arab Eyes by Amin Maalouf (Al-Saqi, 1984).

Islamic Science and Engineering by Donald R Hill (Edinburgh University Press, 1993).

A History of Arab People by Albert Hourani (Faber and Faber, 1991).

The Venture of Islam Marshall Hodgson (Chicago University Press, 1974, 3 vols).

Contacts

AOTEAROA/NEW ZEALAND
International Muslim
Association of New Zealand
PO Box 3101, Wellington
Tel: + 644 387 4226
Email: iman@paradise.net.nz

AUSTRALIA
The Australian Federation of
Islamic Councils
PO Box 1185, Waterloo DC NSW
2017
Tel: + 61 2 9319 6733
Fax: + 61 2 9319 0159
Email: afichalal@bigpond.com

CANADA
Canadian Islamic Congress
Suite 424, 420 Erb St W
Waterloo N2L 6K6
Tel: + 1 519 746 1242
Email: cic@cicnow.com

Canadian Muslim Civil Liberties
Association
885 Progress Ave. UPH 14, Toronto
M1H 3G3
Tel: + 1 416 289 3871
Fax: + 1 416 289 0339

IRELAND
The Islamic Foundation of
Ireland
163 South Circular Road, Dublin 8
Tel: + 353 453 3242
Email: ifi@indigo.ie

UK
Muslim Council of Britain
PO Box 52
Wembley, Middlesex HA9 OXW
Tel: + 44 20 8903 9024
Email: admin@mcb.org.uk

The Islamic Foundation
Markfield Conference Centre
Ratby Lane, Markfield
Leicester LE67 9SY
Tel: + 44 1530 244 944
Email: info@islamic-
foundation.org.uk

US
Islamic Society of North
America
PO Box 38
Plainfields, IN 46168
Tel: + 1 317 839 8157
Email: info@isna.org

American Muslim Council
1212 New York Avenue
NW Suit 400, Washington DC
20005-6102
Tel: + 1 202 789 2262
Email: amc.dc@ix.netcomcom

The Council of American-
Islamic Relations
453 New Jersey Avenue SE,
Washington DC 20003-4034
Tel: + 1 202 488 8787
Email: webmaster@cair-net.org

Index

Bold page numbers refer to main subjects of boxed text.

139

Index

Index

Index